Computerised payroll skills

Debbie Board

Published by Osborne Books Limited
Unit 1B Everoak Estate
Bromyard Road, Worcester WR2 5HP
Tel 01905 748071
Email books@osbornebooks.co.uk
Website www.osbornebooks.co.uk

Design by Laura Ingham

Printed by CPI Group (UK) Limited, Croydon, CR0 4YY, on environmentally friendly, acid-free paper from managed forests.

British Library Cataloguing in Publication Data
A catalogue record for this book is available from the British Library

ISBN 978 1909173 576

Contents

Acknowledgements

The publisher wishes to thank the following for their help with the editing, reading and production of the book: Liz Lay, Cathy Turner and Jon Moore. Thanks are also due to Laura Ingham for her designs for this series.

The publisher is indebted to the Association of Accounting Technicians for its help and advice to our author and editors during the preparation of this text.

Author

Debbie Board spent twenty-six years in the commercial sector before becoming a teacher and assessor of accounting in further education. While working in the commercial sector she was responsible as director and office manager for the introduction of computerised accounting in a multi-million pound business. After thirteen years working as an AAT tutor and running the accounts of an independent tool hire company, she now works as an accounting consultant and writer.

Introduction

what this book covers

This book has been written specifically to cover the 'Computerised payroll skills' Unit which is mandatory for the AAT Level 2 Diploma in Accounting and Business.

The book contains clear and practical explanations of how to set up and run a Sage 50 Payroll system. The Sage system (Version 20) has been chosen as it is widely used both by businesses and by training providers.

A Case Study (Lock Supplies), which demonstrates the processing of a weekly payroll, runs through the chapters. It includes setting up and amending a payroll system, processing weekly payrolls, dealing with new employees and leavers, dealing with deductions, backing up data and producing reports.

There are Student Activities at the end of each chapter, based on the Lock Supplies Case Study data, containing inputting tasks designed to develop the skills needed to process computerised payroll.

A further practice exercise for a different business (Sound Design) is included at the end of the book to help students prepare for the assessment.

a note on tax years

The examples and activities in the text use settings based on the 2014-15 tax year (Finance Act 2014) but the content demonstrates general principles and processes that apply in any tax year.

1 Introduction to computerised payroll

this chapter covers...

This short chapter summarises how computerised payroll is demonstrated in the text.

It describes some of the skills and characteristics required of a payroll administrator.

It includes tips for tutors who use the activities in this text to deliver computerised payroll courses. It covers the treatment of RTI (Real Time Information) and how to enter or change tax and National Insurance settings to suit the tax year in which the data is set.

This chapter also explains how to navigate Sage 50 Payroll software.

INTRODUCTION

This book has been written to cover the Computerised payroll skills Unit of the AAT Level 2 Diploma in Accounting and Business qualification.

It contains clear and practical explanations of how to set up and run a computerised payroll.

Sage 50 Payroll software has been used to demonstrate the use of payroll software as it is widely used by businesses and training providers.

The text shows the use of Sage 50 Payroll for the tax year 2014-15 (Version 20), but the data and practice activities can be applied to any tax year.

A Case Study (Lock Supplies), demonstrating a weekly payroll, runs through the chapters. It is operated by Jay Novak. The Case Study includes:

- setting up the payroll system part-way through the financial year
- setting up records for five existing employees
- processing four weekly payrolls – tax weeks 9 to 12
- dealing with new employees and leavers
- dealing with mandatory deductions such as court orders
- dealing with voluntary deductions such as donating to charity
- amending business and employee records
- backing up data
- producing reports

The Student Activities at the end of each chapter contain inputting tasks designed to develop skills necessary in processing computerised payroll. The activities are based on the Case Study data.

A further practice exercise for a different business (Sound Design) is included at the end of the book. This closely follows the format and content of the AAT's sample assessment and includes a payroll that is run fortnightly rather than weekly.

THE JOB OF PAYROLL ADMINISTRATOR

It is now compulsory for almost all businesses to run their payrolls on computer. The introduction of Real Time Information (RTI) in 2013, with its need for regular online submissions to HMRC, has increased the demand for trained and qualified staff who can operate payroll software.

RTI requires computer software to be compatible with and to communicate with the government's HMRC computer so that employee information such as pay, compulsory deductions, new starter details and leaver details can be updated regularly.

Many commercial payroll software programs are available including HMRC's free Basic Tools software, designed for businesses with fewer than 10 employees. In the Case Study example shown in this text, Sage 50 Payroll is used to demonstrate procedures which are common to all computerised payroll programs. Once you have learned how to use one brand, you will be able to find your way around any payroll software because the tasks involved are the same.

The payroll administrator must also possess the characteristics essential to anyone working in accounts or payroll: an understanding of the need for accuracy, timeliness, and the importance of keeping both data and personal information secure and confidential. The possession of these characteristics together with skills involved in running computerised payroll will increase employability and employment opportunities.

TAX AND NATIONAL INSURANCE SETTINGS

Real Time Information (RTI)

Although regular submission of RTI is now mandatory for business payrolls, it is not necessary to set up any RTI links to HMRC for the purposes of working through the practice exercises in this book. The text does not include any instructions on how to set up links or make submissions.

tax year settings

The examples shown in this text – Case Study, screenshots and reports – are set in the tax year 2014-15. This means that the default PAYE tax and NI bands and rates and other parameters are set to those legally prevailing in the tax year 2014-15.

If using a different tax year, the dates and values calculated may differ from those shown in the text. For example, tax, National Insurance and net pay values may differ and the processing dates may not match the day of the week shown in this text. If payday is a Friday, then in 2014 Week 9 payday would fall on 6 June, whereas in 2013 it would fall on 7 June.

If the process date is set to a date in a previous tax year, the parameters and rates applicable for that year will automatically be applied. For example, if you enter any date in the 2013-14 tax year, the tax band for basic rate tax at 20% was from zero to £32,010 of taxable pay. See the screenshot opposite. To check or amend parameters, go to Company/Legislation on the vertical toolbar.

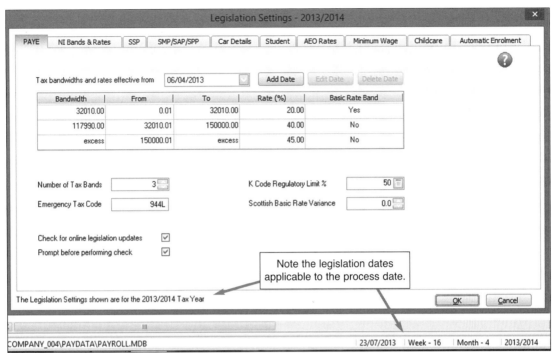

Note the legislation dates applicable to the process date.

If the process date is set to a date in the 2014-15 tax year then the settings for that year automatically apply. In this case the 20% tax band width is zero to £31,865. See the screenshot below.

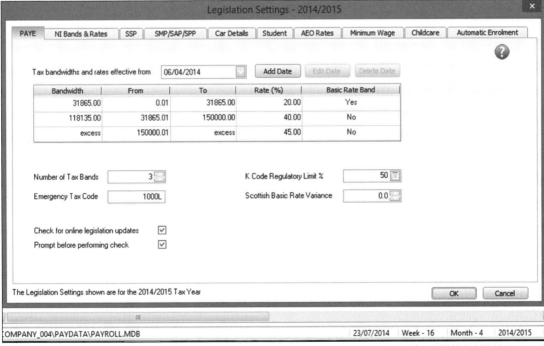

If you set future dates, the latest rates in the software will be applied. For example, if you decide to use dates in the tax year 2015-16 using software purchased for the 2014-15 tax year, the rates will be those from 2014-15. A warning will come up on the screen as shown below.

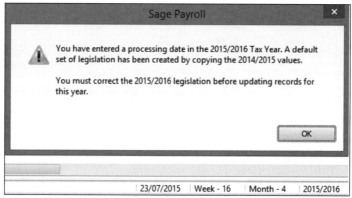

Below are the NI settings that would be applied for the 2015-16 tax year using 2014-15 software.

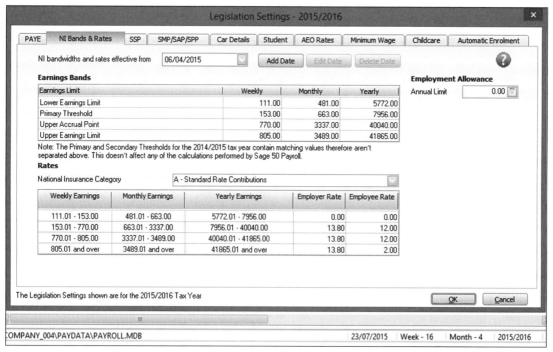

If you need to amend the default settings manually, you can do so.

NAVIGATION

Sage offers various 'views' of the data. You can switch between them using the Change View button. It is a matter of personal preference which you use so have a look at the choices.

This is the 'Payroll Process' view.

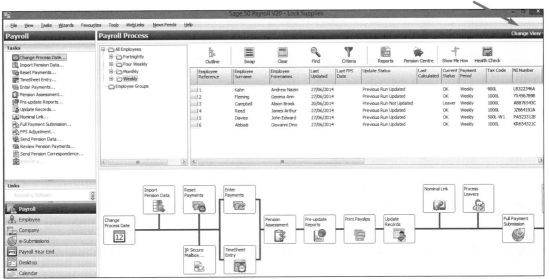

This is the 'Employee List' view which will be used throughout the text.

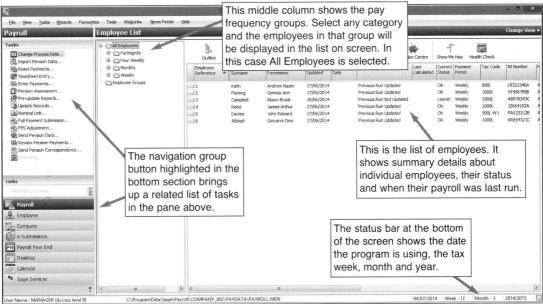

This middle column shows the pay frequency groups. Select any category and the employees in that group will be displayed in the list on screen. In this case All Employees is selected.

The navigation group button highlighted in the bottom section brings up a related list of tasks in the pane above.

This is the list of employees. It shows summary details about individual employees, their status and when their payroll was last run.

The status bar at the bottom of the screen shows the date the program is using, the tax week, month and year.

2 Setting up business details

this chapter covers...

This chapter explains how to set up the program to suit your business. We look at entering:

- business details such as company name, address and HMRC references

- pay rates used for more than one employee

- pension schemes

We also look at how to safeguard data that has been input by backing up.

SETTING UP BUSINESS DETAILS

To start with, you must set up the details of your business. Some of this information is compulsory and you won't be able to proceed unless certain elements are input. For example, the business tax reference and accounts office reference must be included.

The requirement for regular updating of payroll information to HMRC through RTI, means that the accuracy of the information you enter here is vital. If you are submitting real information (making 'submissions') your payroll program will not communicate with HMRC unless it is set up properly.

Throughout this book a Case Study is used to demonstrate computerised payroll in operation. It features a fictitious business, Lock Supplies, which uses Sage 50 Payroll computer software.

Case Study

Jay Novak has taken on payroll administration for Lock Supplies. Lock Supplies' payroll information is as follows:

- all staff work a minimum of 35 hours per week
- for staff paid at an hourly rate, any hours worked above 35 hours are paid at overtime rate
- other staff are paid a flat salary regardless of hours worked
- the payroll is run weekly
- all employees are paid by credit transfer direct to their bank accounts

To enter the business information, Jay clicks on File on the menu bar and then on New Company.

Note: Sage calls a business a 'company'.

The New Company Wizard appears.

Jay clicks Next to create a new set of data files.

She enters the following Company details:

Lock Supplies, Unit 43, Westdown Industrial Estate, Bristol Road, Bath, BA1 7QJ

Tax Dist. / Ref. 034 / S650

Accounts Office Ref. 034 / PB00011122

Jay clicks Next and Finish when she has checked the details are correct.

Now the Change Process Date window appears. The date shown initially will be today's date.

Jay changes it to 6 June 2014 (format 06/06/14) as this is the first payday we are going to use.

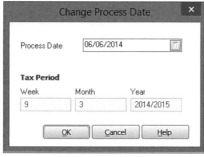

Note that the tax week and month numbers are shown below the date, here Tax Week 9 and Tax Month 3. Jay clicks OK.

The red title bar at the top of the screen now shows the business name, and the Process Date is shown on the status bar at the bottom of the screen together with the relevant tax week and month.

SETTING UP PAY RATES

Once the business details have been set up, the next thing to do is to input any standard pay rates or pay bands used by your business so that they can be applied to your employees. There may be set rates for certain jobs.

Jay must set up some standard rates of pay so that they can then be applied to any employees.

She clicks on the Company button in the vertical toolbar then on Pay Elements in the Tasks list above.

Tip – Tasks list

The Tasks list changes according to which navigation group button you have clicked in the bottom section.

The Pay Elements Settings window appears.

On the Payments tab Jay clicks the New button…

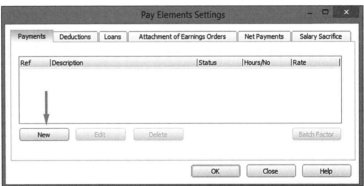

© 2014 Sage (UK) Limited. All rights reserved.

…and enters the following information:

Reference	1
Status	Fixed
Description	Office Supervisor Basic
Default hours	0
Rate	9.00

Jay leaves all the other settings as they are and clicks OK.

Now she adds a second pay band for Office Supervisor Overtime.

Reference	2
Status	Fixed
Description	Office Supervisor Overtime
Default hours	0
Rate	13.50

Then she adds other rates by clicking the New button and entering more details in the same way.

Ref	Pay bands	Basic hourly rate £ per hour	Ref	Overtime hourly rate £ per hour
3	Office assistant	7.00	4	10.50
5	Warehouse staff	8.00	6	12.00

Once all six pay rates have been entered, the screen looks like this:

Finally, Jay clicks OK to leave the Pay Elements Settings window.

SETTING UP A PENSION SCHEME

As with RTI, it is soon going to be compulsory for businesses to operate pension schemes for their employees and to include pension contributions in the payroll. Many businesses already do this.

Pension contributions can be made by the employee or by both the employee and the employer. Any contributions are assigned to individual employees, and a record of contributions made by or on behalf of each member of the scheme is kept by the business. The value of contributions collected for each employee is paid over on a regular basis to the pension company by the business.

For pension contributions to be processed via the payroll, the company providing the pension scheme ('pension provider') must be approved by the government. Any money invested in the scheme is protected until the employee's pension age when the accrued (accumulated) benefits are paid out.

Case Study

The company offers membership of a Group Personal Pension scheme to all employees.

To set up the details, Jay sets the process date to 31 May 2014 by clicking on Payroll and Change Process Date on the vertical toolbar. By using this date, any later pay dates will capture the pension information.

She clicks on Pension Schemes in the task options of the Company navigation group. The Pension Schemes window appears. Some skeleton schemes are partially set up; these can be personalised to Lock Supplies.

Jay clicks Edit and fills in the following:

Details tab

Reference	1
Description	Main scheme
Type	GPP
Qualifying scheme	Yes
Minimum employment period	0 months
Other fields	Leave blank

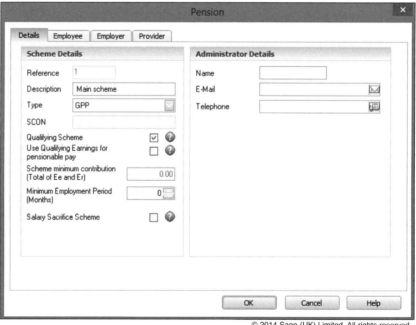

Employee tab

Percentage 3%

'Apply to all Pensionable Earnings' is checked

Minimum and maximum boxes are left at zero

Under Settings, the defaults are left

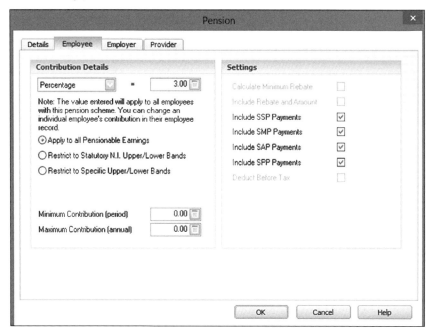

Employer tab

Percentage 2%

There are no other entries on this tab

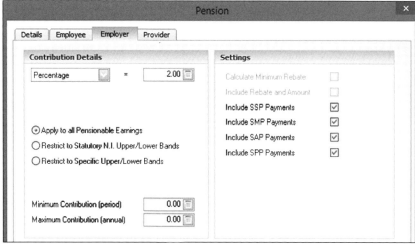

Provider tab

Jay enters the details of the company that provides the pension:

Gennerus Insurance, 17 Thomas Street, Bristol, BS1 4TW

Provider's ref: GI444
Scheme ref: GIB1234

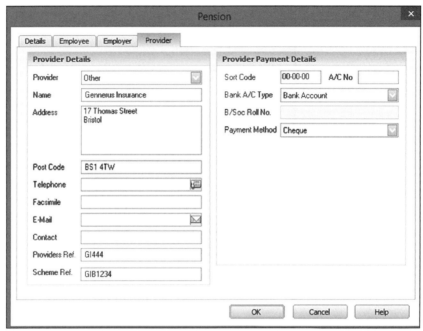

Now she clicks OK to save the information she has entered about the main scheme and then closes the Pension Schemes window.

BACKING UP

Once you have entered a significant amount of data, it is a good idea to safeguard it. This means that if the information was lost for any reason – computer error, flood, fire, theft, corruption – you could retrieve and reload it.

As with any computer program, you should backup regularly. The penalty for not doing so is that if data is lost you would have to input all the information again. So, backup at the end of every session or whenever you have entered new information.

The computer program may name a backup file automatically but you can overwrite it with your own name and save the backup file in a location of your choice, for example on a USB stick.

A backup file is a copy of the data within the payroll program at the time the backup is taken. It does not remove the data in the software, nor does it need to be reloaded unless the main data is lost. Taking a backup makes no difference to how you proceed in using the software. It is simply a safeguard. A backup file can be restored (reloaded) if ever needed.

Case Study

Jay clicks File (on the menu bar) and Backup. The Backup Wizard window appears. She clicks Next. Jay changes the settings so that only 'Data Files' is highlighted.

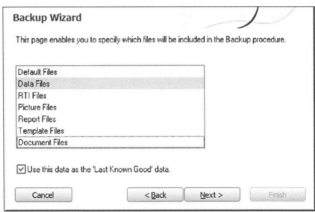

She clicks Next.

Now she needs to identify where the backup file is to be saved so she clicks Browse to choose the location (this could be an external drive).

Although Sage has given the file a name, Jay changes the default filename to **Lock set up** and clicks Save.

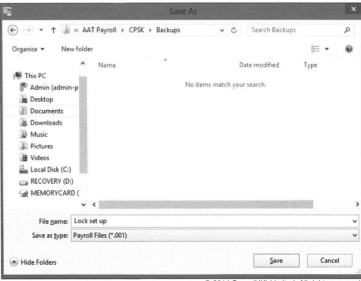

Now Jay is returned to the Backup Wizard. She clicks Next and then Finish. The backup process is visible on the screen.

When it is complete, 'The backup has been successful.' appears on screen. Jay can now click OK.

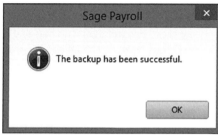

Chapter Summary

■ Before the payroll program can be used, information about the business including name, address and tax office reference must be set up. Sage calls a business a 'company'.

■ Pay rates for different jobs within the business can be set up. This is useful when more than one employee has the same pay rate or pay rates, eg waiter/waitress or shop assistant.

■ If there is an existing company pension scheme, details should be entered at the setting up stage. Some businesses, like the Case Study example, already offer membership of a pension scheme to their employees. Soon it will be compulsory for all businesses to do this.

■ Safeguarding computer data is always important, but never more so than for payroll data. Regular backups are vital.

Key Terms	payroll	a detailed record of amounts paid to employees within a given period
	RTI	Real Time Information. The requirement for businesses to submit payroll information online to HMRC. Submissions must be made on or before each payday
	tax year	the period between 6 April one year and 5 April the next, eg tax year 2014-15 is 6 April 2014 to 5 April 2015
	tax month	the number of the month within the tax year. A tax month is from 6th of one calendar month to 5th of the next, eg Month 9 is 6 December to 5 January
	tax week	the number of the week within the tax year. Week 1 is from 6 April to 12 April. Week 2 from 13 April to 19 April and so on. There can be 53 weeks in each tax year
	pay frequency	the period between paydays. For example, a week (weekly), a fortnight (fortnightly) or a month (monthly)
	process date	the date of the payroll (payday) or the date set for inputting data if different, eg year-to-date figures
	pay elements	pay rates and deductions
	basic	pay or pay rate that is agreed as a normal minimum
	overtime	pay or pay rate that is paid at a higher rate than basic pay usually for working extra hours or unsocial hours
	pension scheme	a system for collecting contributions on behalf of an employee towards their retirement income
	pensionable earnings	the pay on which a percentage contribution to a pension scheme is based. This may be only basic pay or it may be all pay
	pension provider	the company that the business pays pension contributions to for safe-keeping and investment
	backing up	copying the data in the software program at a point in time so that it could be reloaded if necessary

Activities

Use the information and data given in the Case Study to work through the student activities. The relevant page number is given in brackets.

1   Set up the business details for Lock Supplies* (pages 9-10)

2   Set up the six pay rates (pages 11-13)

3   Set up the pension scheme (pages 13-16)

4   Back up (pages 16-18)

*In a training centre where several students are working together and sharing a printer, students could add their name after the business name so that their work is clearly identified. For example, Lock Supplies (Sam White).

3 Employee records

this chapter covers...

Now that basic company information has been set up, details of the workforce can be added. In this chapter we describe how to:

■ *set up records for employees*

■ *set pay frequency*

In the last chapter we looked at backing up data. Here we show how to restore (reload) a backup file when data has been lost.

Finally we cover the production of paper reports, including payslips, and how to capture a screenshot. These skills are vital both for day-to-day payroll operation and for taking payroll examinations.

SETTING UP EMPLOYEE RECORDS

You can now set up the records of all your employees. You can do this at any time during the tax year. The tax year is the 12 months from April 6th one year to April 5th the following year, eg 6 April 2014 to 5 April 2015. As a legal minimum you must have the following information for each member of staff:

- full name (including a middle name if there is one)
- gender (male or female)
- date of birth
- full address
- National Insurance number
- the date the employment started

In practice you will probably fill in other fields in the employee record when you complete their details, eg employee number, telephone number.

Case Study

Jay must now set up the details of the five existing employees from their employee record cards.

There are two ways she could enter employee records:

- a wizard, which takes you through each different element of the employee's details screen by screen – this is not ideal if you want to skip some details
- a 'quick employee' option where you enter all the important details on one screen

Jay chooses to use the second option so she clicks on Employee and Quick Employee on the vertical toolbar.

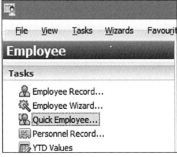

She enters details of the first employee, the business owner: Andrew Kahn.

She can use the Tab key to move from one field to the next and the Next/Back button to move between windows.

Note: in this practice scenario, not all details about the employee are necessary so some fields will be left blank, eg telephone numbers and bank details.

EMPLOYEE RECORD CARD

Reference	1	Payment Method	Credit transfer
Works Number	Not used	Payment Frequency	Weekly
Title	Mr	Employee provided form	None, existing employee
Surname	Kahn		
Forenames	Andrew Nazim	Tax Code	900L
Address	42 Burgess Close Long Ashton Bristol	Week 1/Month 1	Leave blank
		NI Number	LB322346A
		NI Category	A
Postcode	BS41 9PY	Deduct Student Loan	No
Marital Status	Married	Pension Scheme	1 Main scheme
Sex	Male	Department	No department
Date of Birth	09/01/66	Job title	Owner
Employee Start Date	01/10/11	Gross salary	£36000 per year

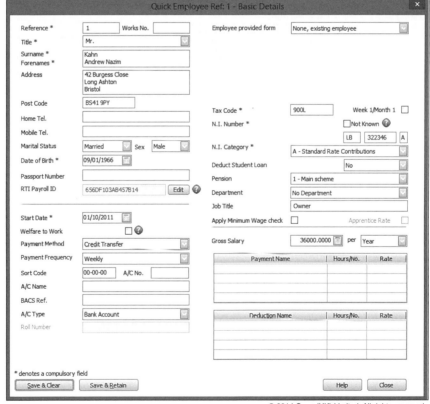

Once Jay has entered all the details for Andrew Kahn, she clicks Save and Clear.

She is now ready to enter the next employee using the same process.

EMPLOYEE RECORD CARD			
Reference	2	Employee provided form	None, existing employee
Works Number	Not used		
Title	Ms	Tax Code	1000L
Surname	Fleming	Week1/Month 1	Leave blank
Forenames	Gemma Ann	NI Number	YX456789B
Address	4 Manor Drive Keynsham Bristol	NI Category	A
		Deduct Student Loan	No
		Pension Scheme	1 Main scheme
Postcode	BS31 4LS	Department	No department
Marital Status	Single	Job title	Office supervisor
Sex	Female	Gross salary	Leave blank
Date of Birth	17/07/64	Payment name	1 Office supervisor basic
Employee Start Date	01/10/11		
Payment Method	Credit transfer	Payment name	2 Office supervisor overtime
Payment Frequency	Weekly		

© 2014 Sage (UK) Limited. All rights reserved.

Tip – Ways of entering pay details for an employee

On the employee record form, there is a place for entering a Gross Salary and below it, Payment Name and Deduction Name. If a gross salary is entered here the same value will be calculated automatically each payday. If an employee works variable hours or has more than one rate of pay then enter the details under Payment Name.

There are now two employee records on the screen in the right hand window. Some information is hidden to the right of the screen. Jay can use the horizontal scroll bar at the bottom to see all the details.

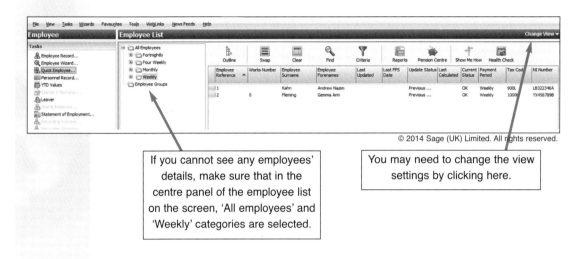

If you cannot see any employees' details, make sure that in the centre panel of the employee list on the screen, 'All employees' and 'Weekly' categories are selected.

You may need to change the view settings by clicking here.

Jay now enters the remaining employees from the details shown below. Only the details that need to be input are given. All staff are paid weekly by credit transfer and are existing employees. All are NI letter A.

EMPLOYEE RECORD CARD			
Reference	3	Employee Start Date	01/10/11
Title	Miss	Tax Code	1000L
Surname	Campbell	Week1/Month 1?	No
Forenames	Alison Brook	NI Number	AB876543C
Address	Flat 3	Deduct Student Loan	No
	St Annes House	Pension Scheme	No pension scheme
	St Annes	Job title	Office assistant
	Bristol		
Postcode	BS4 4KK	Payment Names	3 Office assistant
Sex	Female		basic
Date of Birth	05/03/88		4 Office assistant overtime

EMPLOYEE RECORD CARD				
Reference	4	Employee Start Date	15/04/12
Title	Mr	Tax Code	1000L
Surname	Reed	Week1/Month 1	No
Forenames	James Arthur	NI Number	JZ664192A
Address	8 Newton Lane Bristol Road Bath	NI Category	A
		Pension Scheme	1 Main scheme
		Job title	Sales representative
Postcode	BA1 7TD	Gross salary	£24,000 per year
Sex	Male		
Date of Birth	24/01/67		

EMPLOYEE RECORD CARD				
Reference	5	Employee Start Date	01/10/11
Title	Mr	Tax Code	856L
Surname	Davies	Week1/Month 1	No
Forenames	John Edward	NI Number	PA523312B
Address	188 London Road Bathampton Bath	NI Category	A
		Pension Scheme	No pension scheme
		Job title	Warehouse operative
Postcode	BA2 6GE	Payment Names	5 Warehouse basic
Sex	Male		6 Warehouse overtime
Date of Birth	01/11/56		

PAY FREQUENCY

In the Case Study the employees are paid once a week. In addition to weekly payroll, you can set the program to pay fortnightly (every two weeks), every four weeks or monthly. For a large business, there may be different pay intervals for different groups of employees.

Where you enter a gross salary in the employee record, it is converted by the program to suit the pay period. For example, if you enter an annual salary and the pay is weekly, then the program automatically calculates the weekly pay as the annual salary divided by 52.

Once the details of all your existing employees have been set up, it is likely that you may want to check some of the details. You will also need to know how to revisit employee records from time to time once the payroll is running.

Case Study

Now there are five employees of Lock Supplies on the screen.

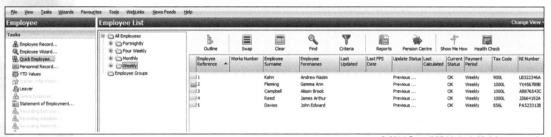

Jay can use the scroll bar at the bottom of the screen to see more information about the employees.

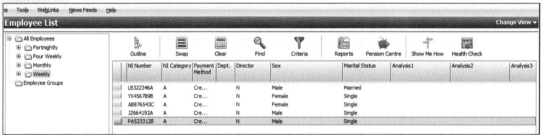

If she wants to return to individual details of any of the employees, perhaps to change something or just to check it, she can select the employee and then click Employee Record (top left of the screen), or she can just double-click the employee name. The Quick Employee form does not appear again (this can only be used once before saving), but all the details that have been entered are kept within the employee record.

Each record includes ten tabs where information about and history of the employee is held.

Jay wants to check the records of all employees in turn so she selects all of them in the Employee List. She does this by clicking Swap on the toolbar, then clicking Employee Record (top left of the screen again).

First she sees the Personal tab for reference 1 employee, Andrew Kahn.

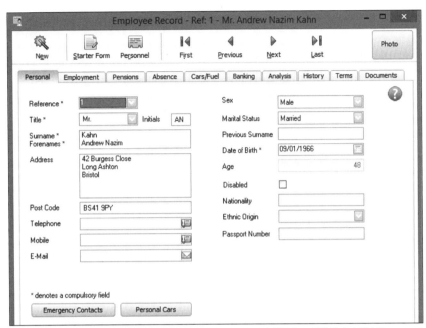

Jay can move between the various employees by using the navigation buttons at the top of the record – First, Previous, Next and Last. She clicks Next and is taken to the next employee record (from those selected). In this case, number 2, Gemma Fleming.

This time Jay clicks on Gemma's Employment tab. Here are details relevant to Gemma's employment including a button leading to her pay elements.

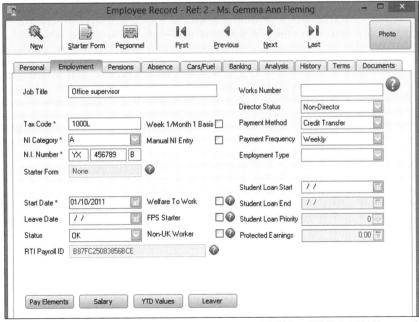

Jay clicks Next again to look at Employee 3, Alison Campbell. She clicks on her Pensions tab. She notices that this shows that there is 'no Pension scheme set'. If Jay uses the Previous arrow button to go back to Gemma Fleming's record, she will see that on Gemma's Pension tab the Main scheme is shown. If an existing employee wanted to join the pension scheme, she could click on Manage Schemes here and add details.

Tip – Look at the other tabs

None of the other tabs have been used yet, but you can have a look at them and you can practise moving between selected employees using the navigation buttons.

When Jay returns to the main Employee List screen, she clicks on Clear to remove the selection.

RESTORING AND RECOVERING DATA

You may need to reload a backup file at some time. For example, when data has been lost or accidentally over-written or when you want to return to an earlier date and start again.

Restoring a backup file will use the data copied at the time of the backup and reload it into the program. The restored file will overwrite any other data currently in the program so the process of restoring should be used with care.

Tip – Restoring and recovering

Sage distinguishes between reloading data that has been backed up deliberately and data that has been backed up automatically as part of the payroll run process. It calls the first one 'restoring' and the second one 'recovering'.

In case Jay needed to reload one of her own backup files at any time, here is the procedure she would follow.

It is not advisable to follow this procedure at this stage without backing up the employee records. They will be lost in the restore and you would have to input them again.

1. Click File and Restore. The Restore Wizard opens.

2. Select the file to be restored (use the scroll bar to see all the details). Click Next and follow the prompts. If it is not displayed click Next twice and use the Browse button to find the required file. Click Finish to start the Restore process.

3. Once the Restore is complete confirm the process date and click OK.

If Jay wanted to reload an automatic backup, she would choose Recover from the File menu and follow the Recover Wizard instructions. These are similar to those for Restore above.

PRODUCING REPORTS

In spite of the fact that computer programs save a lot of paperwork and store electronic records, you will need to print out some information. For example, you must print out payslips to hand to your employees and you will probably still want to print out some routine reports giving summary information for your paper records.

Jay wants to print a copy of a report showing all employees' personal details. First she makes sure that none of the employees is selected (she can click Clear if necessary).

> **Tip – All or one?**
>
> If you have one or more employees selected when running a report rather than all employees, only the details of selected employees will appear on the report.

Then she clicks on the Reports icon on the horizontal toolbar. The Reports window appears.

She selects Employee in the left hand window and then scrolls down to Employee Details – Personal in the right hand window.

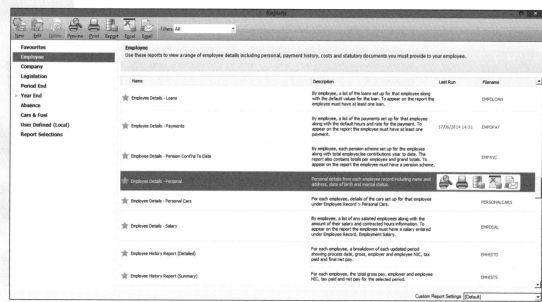

She clicks Preview on the Reports toolbar at the top of the page (or double-clicks the report name) to see how the report will appear.

Tip – Previewing the whole report

You may need to maximise the window to see the report in full. You can control the view by using the Zoom button.

Here Jay can either print the report by clicking Print at the top of the screen or she can save it as a PDF document by clicking Export and choosing where to save it, perhaps for printing at a later time.

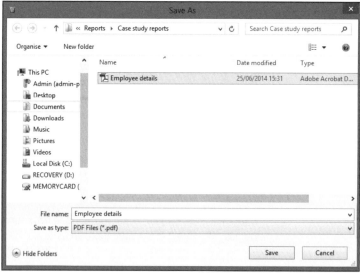

When printed or previewed, the two pages of the report look like this.

Date :											Page :	1 of 2	
Time :				**Lock Supplies**									
				Employee Details - Personal									
				Tax Week 9		Tax Month 3							

Employee Reference	Employee Name, Address, Email & Mobile	Job Title	Employment Status Type	Date of Birth	Marital Status	Sex	Pay Frequency	NI Number	NI Cat	Con Out	Tax Code	W1/ M1	Starter Form	Start Date	Pay Method
1	Andrew Nazim Kahn 42 Burgess Close Long Ashton Bristol BS41 9PY	Owner		09/01/1966	Married	Male	Weekly	LB322346A	A	N	900L	N	None	01/10/2011	Credit Transfer
2	Gemma Ann Fleming 4 Manor Drive Keynsham Bristol BS31 4LS	Office supervisor		17/07/1964	Single	Female	Weekly	YX456789B	A	N	1000L	N	None	01/10/2011	Credit Transfer
3	Alison Brook Campbell Flat 3 St Annes House St Annes Bristol BS4 4KK	Office assistant		05/03/1988	Single	Female	Weekly	AB876543C	A	N	1000L	N	None	01/10/2011	Credit Transfer

Date :											Page :	2 of 2	
Time :				**Lock Supplies**									
				Employee Details - Personal									
				Tax Week 9		Tax Month 3							

Employee Reference	Employee Name, Address, Email & Mobile	Job Title	Employment Status Type	Date of Birth	Marital Status	Sex	Pay Frequency	NI Number	NI Cat	Con Out	Tax Code	W1/ M1	Starter Form	Start Date	Pay Method
4	James Arthur Reed 8 Newton Lane Bristol Road Bath BA1 7TD	Sales representative		24/01/1967	Single	Male	Weekly	JZ664192A	A	N	1000L	N	None	15/04/2012	Credit Transfer
5	John Edward Davies 188 London Road Bathampton Bath BA2 6GE	Warehouse operative		01/11/1956	Single	Male	Weekly	PA523312B	A	N	856L	N	None	01/10/2011	Credit Transfer

Jay can close the Reports window by clicking the X in the top right hand corner of the screen or clicking Close on the menu bar.

TAKING A SCREENSHOT

If you ever need to record or print an image of what you can see on the screen, you can take a screenshot. A screenshot is also referred to as a 'screen grab', 'screen capture' or 'screen dump'.

To take a screenshot when you have an image on the screen that you want to capture, simply press the Print Scr button on your keyboard (or you may have an abbreviation eg 'prt sc'). Then paste it into an open document in your chosen program, eg Word or Paint. You can now print the document and/or save it.

You will need to be able to take a screenshot if you take a payroll assessment. You need to be able to show the assessor what was on your screen. You will get some practice of this in the student activities at the end of this chapter and those that follow.

Chapter Summary

■ A record must be set up for each employee in the workforce. It should include certain personal information – such as name, address and age – as a legal minimum. The employee record will also include job title and pay rate, tax code, pay frequency, method of payment, whether in the pension scheme and whether student loan repayments are to be deducted from pay.

■ For each employee, pay frequency must be set. You can set the payroll to run weekly, fortnightly, every four weeks or monthly. The program will divide a gross salary up to suit the pay period set, eg a monthly payroll would take an annual salary and divide it by 12 for each payday.

■ If data is lost through computer error, flood, fire, theft, corruption or accidental over-writing, or if you just want to return to an earlier date, you can reload a backup file taken earlier. This is done by using the 'restore' or 'recover' function.

■ A range of reports can be printed from the program. These can be in paper form, filed for reference, or they can be saved as PDF computer files.

■ A screenshot is a printed image of what appears on the computer screen. You need to know how to print a screenshot if you are being assessed.

salary	an agreed amount of pay for a time period, eg £2,000 per month or £24,000 per year. Although wages and earnings mean the same thing, the word 'salary' has tended to be used for professional workers
tax code	a code (usually a number and a letter) issued by HMRC denoting how much an employee can receive free of tax in a year. This free pay is spread out over the number of paydays in the year
student loan	an amount loaned to students of universities and colleges by the government to cover expenses including tuition fees. The amount is repayable through the payroll once the student earns above a given threshold
National Insurance	employee and employer contributions towards state benefits in the UK. Usually abbreviated to NI or NIC
NI number	a unique reference allocated to every child in the UK and to anyone from overseas who has a right to work in the UK
NI category	a letter denoting how contributions are calculated dependent on an employee's age and pension arrangements
restoring	reloading data that was saved in a backup file. Restoring overwrites existing data
recovering	the same as restoring but from an automatic backup rather than a deliberate backup
report	a paper copy of data. This can be printed out or saved as a PDF file
screenshot	capturing and saving or printing an image of how the computer screen looks

Activities

Use the information and data given in the Case Study to work through the student activities. The relevant page number is given in brackets.

1   Set up the five employee records (pages 23-27)

2   Run an Employee Details – Personal report (pages 31-32)

3   Take a screenshot showing the backup name (page 34)

     Check your report against the one on page 33

4 The first payroll

this chapter covers...

Now we come to running the first payroll.

Unless the software is used with effect from 6 April, year-to-date values such as gross pay and tax paid to date for each employee must be input.

This chapter shows how to run a payroll and includes preparation as follows:

■ *setting or changing the process date*

■ *entering employee payments*

■ *running pre-update checks and reports*

Once all the information is input and double-checked, the payroll can be 'updated'. We process and finalise the payroll for Week 9.

THE FIRST PAYROLL

You have set up your employee records by entering their basic personal details and information. Now you can add some more information to enable you to run the first payroll.

YEAR-TO-DATE VALUES

Unless you start the payroll on 6 April, you will have to enter year-to-date (YTD) values for each existing employee. This includes the amount of gross pay each employee has received since 6 April in the current year together with the tax and National Insurance that has been deducted.

Case Study

Because Jay is starting to run the computerised payroll part-way through a tax year (from Week 9), she must first enter year-to-date (YTD) values for each employee. These values are the amounts that have been generated previously in the tax year.

Week 8 includes all the previous figures. Payday of that week was Friday 30 May so Jay sets the computer date to 30 May (Payroll/Change Process Date on the vertical toolbar) and enters the YTD values.

First she selects all the employees by clicking Swap. Then she clicks Employee and YTD values on the vertical toolbar.

Using the table below, she works through all the employees, entering the data as shown for each of them. A screenshot of Andrew Kahn's entry is shown on the next page.

Employee	Gross pay (all) £	Tax paid £	Up to LEL £	LEL to PT* £	ET to UAP £	UAP to UEL £	Ee NIC £	Er NIC £
A Kahn	5,538.46	830.40	888.00	336.00	4,314.46	0.00	517.74	595.40
G Fleming	2,628.00	217.60	888.00	336.00	1,404.00	0.00	168.48	193.75
A Campbell	2,023.00	96.00	888.00	336.00	799.00	0.00	95.88	110.26
J Reed	3,692.31	430.40	888.00	336.00	2,468.31	0.00	296.20	340.63
J Davies	2,432.00	222.40	888.00	336.00	1,208.00	0.00	144.96	166.70

*Note that Sage sometimes uses the term ET (Earnings Threshold) instead of PT (Primary Threshold). The figure is the same.

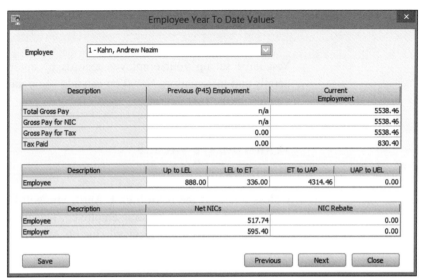

Jay can now print a report showing YTD values entered. She makes sure the date is still set to 30 May then clicks Reports above the Employee List. Under the Employee range, she finds Employee Details – Cumulative. She selects it, previews it to check it and then exports and saves it as a PDF.

Date :						Lock Supplies					Page :		1 of 1			
Time :						Employee Details - Cumulative										
						Tax Week 8		Tax Month 2								

E'ee Ref	Employee Name	SSP	SMP	SPP	SAP	Total Gross	NI'able Earns TD	Taxable Pay	Tax Due To Date	Student Loan	Holiday Fund	Employee NI	Employer NI	Loans	Employee Pension	Employer Pension
1	Mr. AN Kahn	0.00	0.00	0.00	0.00	5538.46	5538.46	5538.46	830.40	0.00	0.00	517.74	595.40	0.00	0.00	0.00
2	Ms. GA Fleming	0.00	0.00	0.00	0.00	2628.00	2628.00	2628.00	217.60	0.00	0.00	168.48	193.75	0.00	0.00	0.00
3	Miss. AB Campbell	0.00	0.00	0.00	0.00	2023.00	2023.00	2023.00	96.00	0.00	0.00	95.88	110.26	0.00	0.00	0.00
4	Mr. JA Reed	0.00	0.00	0.00	0.00	3692.31	3692.31	3692.31	430.40	0.00	0.00	296.20	340.63	0.00	0.00	0.00
5	Mr. JE Davies	0.00	0.00	0.00	0.00	2432.00	2432.00	2432.00	222.40	0.00	0.00	144.96	166.70	0.00	0.00	0.00
	Totals :	0.00	0.00	0.00	0.00	16313.77	16313.77	16313.77	1796.80	0.00	0.00	1223.26	1406.74	0.00	0.00	0.00

She needs a bit more detail about the NIC values to date, so she locates a different report: NI contributions – TD. She previews this one and saves it as a PDF.

Date :							Lock Supplies						Page :		1 of 1	
Time :							NI Contributions - TD									
							Tax Week : 8	Tax Month : 2								

Reference & Name		Current Category	Earnings To LEL	Earnings To PT	Earnings To UAP	Earnings To UEL	NIC Earnings	Gross for NIC	Employee Contribution	Employee Rebate	Employer Contribution	Employer Rebate	Total Contribution	Total Rebate
1	AN Kahn	A	888.00	336.00	4314.46	0.00	5,538.46	5,538.46	517.74	0.00	595.40	0.00	1,113.14	0.00
2	GA Fleming	A	888.00	336.00	1404.00	0.00	2,628.00	2,628.00	168.48	0.00	193.75	0.00	362.23	0.00
3	AB Campbell	A	888.00	336.00	799.00	0.00	2,023.00	2,023.00	95.88	0.00	110.26	0.00	206.14	0.00
4	JA Reed	A	888.00	336.00	2468.31	0.00	3,692.31	3,692.31	296.20	0.00	340.63	0.00	636.83	0.00
5	JE Davies	A	888.00	336.00	1208.00	0.00	2,432.00	2,432.00	144.96	0.00	166.70	0.00	311.66	0.00
			£4,440.00	£1,680.00	£10193.77	£0.00	£16,313.77	£16,313.77	£1,223.26	£0.00	£1,406.74	£0.00	£2,630.00	£0.00

Tip – Report favourites

There are lots of different reports in Sage 50 Payroll. You are unlikely to use them all. In fact, you are likely only to use a small range of reports each time you run the payroll. You can mark your most frequently run reports as 'favourites' by clicking the grey star by the report as shown below and turning it yellow.

This copies that report into the Favourites file so you can find it there in future instead of trawling through a long list every time you need it.

Jay is now ready to process the first payroll.

CHANGING THE PROCESS DATE

First, check the process date. It must be the day you are going to pay your employees – traditionally known as 'payday'. Change the date if necessary.

On the vertical toolbar, Jay clicks on Payroll and Change Process Date.

The Change Process Date window appears.

She changes the date to Friday of Week 9 (06/06/2014) and notes how Sage displays the corresponding tax period below, ie Week 9, Month 3, year 2014/2015. She clicks OK.

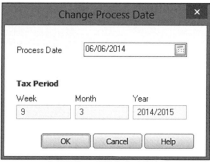

In order to run the payroll she must select the staff to be paid so she clicks on each employee to highlight their records (or she clicks Swap on the toolbar).

Tip – Swap and clear

Swap and Clear help to control the selection of employees. Swap will select all those currently unselected. Clear will deselect any currently selected.

ENTERING PAYMENTS

Select the employees to be paid and then work through each record, entering their pay values as you go, or checking them if they are already set up. You can run this process as often as you need to. If you make a mistake that needs correcting, you can re-enter the details. Nothing is final until you have clicked the Update records command (see page 49).

Statutory deductions such as tax and National Insurance are calculated automatically by the program.

Jay can now start to process the payroll for Week 9.

Employees who are paid an annual salary will automatically have their pay generated by the program. This applies to Andrew Kahn and James Reed. Others are on hourly pay and their hours must be input from their timesheets. This applies to Gemma Fleming, Alison Campbell and John Davies.

Their timesheets show the following hours worked:

Employee	Basic	Overtime	Total
G Fleming	35	4	39
A Campbell	35	0	35
J Davies	35	3	38

Now Jay clicks on Enter Payments (on the vertical toolbar).

Tip – Sage warnings

Various warning windows will pop up from time to time in Sage, some reminding you that you should have done something, some offering you online updates of legislation.

Because you are in a training or practice situation many of these are not relevant, so feel free to disregard them.

Legislation updates can be turned off by clicking Company/Legislation Settings then unchecking 'Check for online legislation updates'.

The Enter Payments window appears showing a summary of the payment for the first employee – Andrew Kahn. His pay has already been generated because a gross salary figure was entered in his employee record at set up. At the bottom, the screen shows the Tax and National Insurance that will be deducted this week and the net pay he will receive.

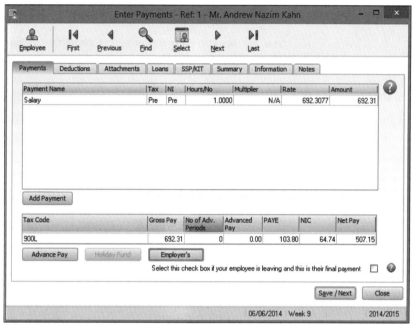

Jay clicks Save/Next to go to Gemma Fleming's payment tab. Jay must input Gemma's hours from the timesheet.

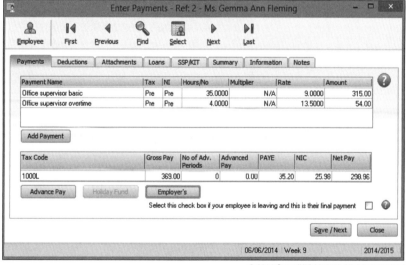

Jay works through each employee's Enter Payments screen (using the navigation arrows) until all employees' pay for Week 9 has been entered.

Tip – Get it right before you update

You can amend payments and re-save them at this stage as many times as you need to – until you get it right! You will not be able to make amendments once you have 'updated records' (see page 49).

At this stage, the only other tab that is of interest when processing payments is the Summary tab. So when Jay has finished entering the payments, she looks back through the individual employee Enter Payments screens but this time she looks at the Summary tabs. Here she sees all payments and deductions recorded, including employee pension contributions where the employee is enrolled on a pension scheme.

Here is James Reed's summary.

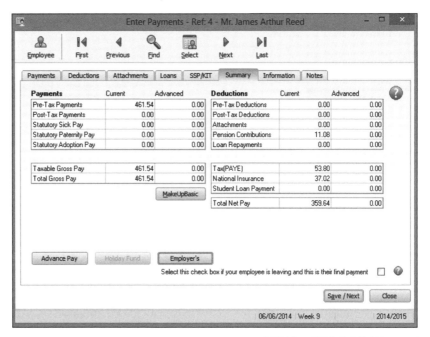

PRE-UPDATE REPORTS

Before you give the final command for the computer to 'update', you can run or save some reports that summarise the current payroll. This is when you print payslips which you are legally required to give to your employees.

Case Study

Now Jay runs some reports.

First she selects all the employees (using Swap). Then she clicks Pre-update Reports on the vertical toolbar. The Reports window appears.

On the left hand tree she clicks Summary and in the right hand window she scrolls down to Update Records Check Report. This report will be used regularly so she clicks the star to make it a favourite for next time.

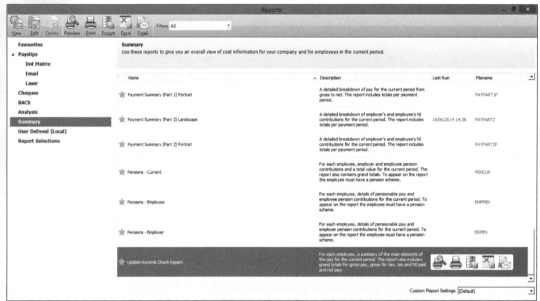

She clicks Preview on the horizontal toolbar to see the report on screen.

Date : Time :		**Lock Supplies**							Page :	1 of 1
		Update Records Check Report								
		Tax Month : 3	Week : 9							

Ref	Name	Payment Method	Payment Frequency	Tax Code	W1/ M1	NI Cat	Total Gross	Taxable Gross	Tax Paid	Employee NIC	Net Pay
1	AN Kahn	Credit Transfer	Weekly	900L	N	A	692.31	692.31	103.80	64.74	507.15
2	GA Fleming	Credit Transfer	Weekly	1000L	N	A	369.00	369.00	35.20	25.98	298.96
3	AB Campbell	Credit Transfer	Weekly	1000L	N	A	245.00	245.00	11.00	11.10	222.90
4	JA Reed	Credit Transfer	Weekly	1000L	N	A	461.54	461.54	53.80	37.02	359.64
5	JE Davies	Credit Transfer	Weekly	856L	N	A	316.00	316.00	30.40	19.62	265.98
							2,083.85	2,083.85	234.20	158.46	1,654.63

This is the time to double-check that all details are correct before putting the payroll into action. If Jay needs to make amendments she can use the Enter Payments option again and then re-run the report.

Jay is happy with the report details so she previews the employees' payslips.

She clicks Pre-update Reports (she may still be in this window), then clicks Payslips and chooses Laser (2 per A4 sheet). She previews the payslips.

Here is Andrew Kahn's payslip. It shows the following:

- Gross pay on the left: £692.31. This is his annual salary of £36,000 divided by 52 to give weekly pay.
- In the middle are his deductions: tax, NI and pension. The employer pension contribution is also shown though not deducted.
- On the right hand side are year-to-date (YTD) figures.
- At the bottom are the pay date, his tax code, his name and his net pay calculated as follows:

Gross pay	£692.31
Less:	
Tax	£103.80
NI	£64.74
Pension	£16.62
Net pay	£507.15

Lock Supplies

Department	-			Payment Method - Credit Transfer		Payment Period - Weekly	
Salary	1.00	692.3077	692.31	PAYE Tax	103.80	Total Gross Pay TD	6230.77
				National Insurance	64.74	Gross for Tax TD	6230.77
				Ee Pension	16.62	Tax paid TD	934.20
				Er Pension	13.85	Earnings For NI TD	6230.46
						National Insurance TD	582.48
						Ee Pension TD	16.62
						Employers Pension TD	13.85
						Earnings for NI	692.00
						Gross for Tax	692.31
						Total Gross Pay	692.31
						Nat. Insurance No	LB322346A
9	06/06/2014			900L	1	Mr. AN Kahn	507.15

And here is John Davies' payslip. His gross pay is made up of his basic hourly pay and overtime, shown on different lines. The only deductions are tax and NI.

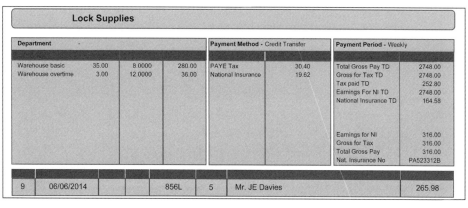

Lock Supplies

Department	-			Payment Method - Credit Transfer		Payment Period - Weekly	
Warehouse basic	35.00	8.0000	280.00	PAYE Tax	30.40	Total Gross Pay TD	2748.00
Warehouse overtime	3.00	12.0000	36.00	National Insurance	19.62	Gross for Tax TD	2748.00
						Tax paid TD	252.80
						Earnings For NI TD	2748.00
						National Insurance TD	164.58
						Earnings for NI	316.00
						Gross for Tax	316.00
						Total Gross Pay	316.00
						Nat. Insurance No	PA523312B
9	06/06/2014			856L	5	Mr. JE Davies	265.98

Finally Jay runs a couple of reports that summarise all the values in the payroll.

She previews a Payment Summary by first clicking Summary and Payment Summary (Part 1) Landscape. Then she repeats the process for Payment Summary (Part 2) Landscape. In the pay period window that comes up, she puts 'is' and 'weekly' in the boxes before clicking OK. She makes them favourites as she will be using these reports again for future payroll runs.

| Date: | | | | | | | Lock Supplies | | | | | | | | Page: | 1 of 1 | | | |
| Time: | | | | | | | Payment Summary (Part 1) Landscape | | | | | | | | | | | | |

Tax Month : 3   Week : 9   Payment Frequency: Weekly

E'ee Ref	Employee Name	Total Gross	Taxable Gross	Pre-Tax Payment	Pre-Tax Ded'n	Student Loan	PAYE	Employee NIC	Employee Pension*	SSP	SMP	SPP	ASPP	SAP	Post-Tax Payment	Post-Tax Ded'n	B/F	C/F	Net Pay
1	AN Kahn	692.31	692.31	692.31	0.00	0.00	103.80	64.74	16.62	0.00	0.00	0.00	0.00	0.00	0.00	0.00	0.00	0.00	507.15
2	GA Fleming	369.00	369.00	369.00	0.00	0.00	35.20	25.98	8.86	0.00	0.00	0.00	0.00	0.00	0.00	0.00	0.00	0.00	298.96
3	AB Campbell	245.00	245.00	245.00	0.00	0.00	11.00	11.10	0.00	0.00	0.00	0.00	0.00	0.00	0.00	0.00	0.00	0.00	222.90
4	JA Reed	461.54	461.54	461.54	0.00	0.00	53.80	37.02	11.08	0.00	0.00	0.00	0.00	0.00	0.00	0.00	0.00	0.00	359.64
5	JE Davies	316.00	316.00	316.00	0.00	0.00	30.40	19.62	0.00	0.00	0.00	0.00	0.00	0.00	0.00	0.00	0.00	0.00	265.98
5	Employees	2083.85	2083.85	2083.85	0.00	0.00	234.20	158.46	36.56	0.00	0.00	0.00	0.00	0.00	0.00	0.00	0.00	0.00	1654.63

*Please note this value does not include any contribution made to a salary sacrifice pension scheme.

| Date: | | | Lock Supplies | | | | | | | Page: | 1 of 1 | | |
| Time: | | | Payment Summary (Part 2) Landscape | | | | | | | | | | |

Tax Month : 3   Week : 9   Payment Frequency: Weekly

E'ee Ref	Employee Name	NI'able Earnings	E'ee + E'er NI Contribution	Employer NI Contribution	Employee NI Contribution	Employer NI Rebate	Employee NI Rebate	Employer Pension*	Tax Code	Week 1 / Month 1	NI Cat	Con Out
1	AN Kahn	692.00	139.19	74.45	64.74	0.00	0.00	13.85	900L	N	A	N
2	GA Fleming	369.00	55.86	29.88	25.98	0.00	0.00	7.38	1000L	N	A	N
3	AB Campbell	245.00	23.86	12.76	11.10	0.00	0.00	0.00	1000L	N	A	N
4	JA Reed	461.00	79.59	42.57	37.02	0.00	0.00	9.23	1000L	N	A	N
5	JE Davies	316.00	42.18	22.56	19.62	0.00	0.00	0.00	856L	N	A	N
5	Employees	£2,083.00	£340.68	£182.22	£158.46	£0.00	£0.00	£30.46				

*For salary sacrifice pension schemes this is the employer contribution including the amount sacrificed by the employee.

She saves them both as PDFs then closes the Reports window.

RUNNING THE PAYROLL – WEEK 9

Once you are happy with all the entries you have made, you can update the payroll. This means you tell the program to use the figures it has calculated to record pay for your employees. At this point the following things are recorded within the program:

What?	Why?
Net pay for each employee	So you know how much money to pay each of them. This is their gross pay less deductions.
Statutory deductions of tax	So you can pay over the correct amount to HMRC.
Statutory deductions for National Insurance: employee (primary) contribution	
Statutory National Insurance: employer (secondary) contribution	
Any student loan repayments	
Other statutory deductions	So that you can pay them over to the correct agency, eg court order payments, council tax arrears.
Non-statutory deductions	So that these can be paid over to the agencies involved, eg pension contributions to the pension provider, charity donations to the charity agency.

Tip – After updating it's too late to change

Once the Payroll has been run, ie the records 'updated', details cannot be changed. If errors are discovered then an earlier backup must be restored or the 'rollback' facility used (see page 85) and the whole payment process run again.

The information generated by the update is stored in the program and used to produce the RTI submission when a real payroll is operated.

Jay selects all employees.

She clicks Update Records on the vertical toolbar. The Sage Payroll warning box appears reminding Jay to run pre-update reports. She has already run them so she just clicks Yes to continue.

The Update Records Wizard appears.

Jay backs up to a specific storage location by using the Backup button. She gives the file her own name. She could allow the default Sage backup name if she preferred.

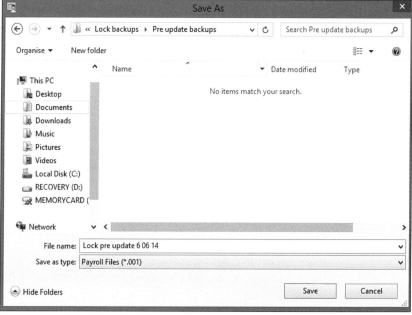

Tip – Filenames

Each time you run the payroll and take a backup, Sage will automatically differentiate the filename by adding the tax week and year. For example, SagePay.Lock Supplies.0914.001 will be the backup for Week 9 in the year 2014. The .001 suffix designates a Sage file. The backup for Week 10 will be SagePay.Lock Supplies.1014.001, and so on. You can rename the file, as Jay has just done, if you wish.

Further on in the wizard, Sage will take an automatic backup which is saved within the program but can be used to recover data if necessary.

Jay clicks Next to proceed through the wizard.

She clicks Finish when she reaches the end. Sage confirms that five records have been updated so Jay clicks OK.

Jay looks at the employee list on the screen and notes that the Last Updated column now shows the date of 6 June.

She has a look at one or two employee records by double-clicking them and clicking the History tab to check summary details of the payments made.

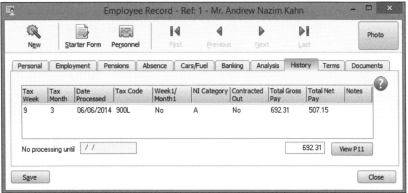

She also clicks View P11 to see a breakdown of tax and NI deductions for individual employees.

Here are the P11 tabs in Andrew Kahn's record.

Tip – Checking arithmetic

Press F2 to bring up a handy on-screen calculator.

Chapter Summary

- If the computerised payroll is being started on the first payday of the tax year, you can run the first payroll straight away. If it is being started part-way through the tax year, you must enter year-to-date pay values for each existing employee.

- It is important that the correct date is set when information is input. The process date must be set or changed whenever data is processed.

- Once all the payroll settings and employee details are set up, including the entry of year-to-date values, the payroll payments for the first payroll run can be entered. When you prepare to run the payroll, you enter or check payments for each employee.

- You can run a pre-update report to check everything is correct before running the payroll.

- When you are sure that the payroll figures are correct and that all eligible employees are being paid, you can 'update records'. That means you run the payroll.

Key Terms	**gross pay**	pay before deductions. Gross pay is made up of basic pay, overtime, bonuses, commission, advanced pay, and statutory payments such as sick pay and maternity pay
	net pay	gross pay less deductions
	employee NIC	Primary Class 1 National Insurance contribution paid by employees through their pay
	employer NIC	Secondary Class 1 National Insurance contribution paid by employers on the pay of their employees
	LEL	Lower Earnings Limit. The level below which no contribution is due and no benefit accrued. Above this level but below the PT benefits are accrued but no contribution is paid
	PT	Primary Threshold. The level at which contributions are due from the employee
	ST	Secondary Threshold. The level at which contributions are due from the employer. In the tax year 2014-15, the level is the same as the PT
	UAP	Upper Accrual Point. The level at which certain rates change, dependent on a range of factors
	UEL	Upper Earnings Limit. The level at which rates change, dependent on a range of factors but different to UAP
	pre-update	the stage at which all payments and deductions have been entered for the workforce, but the payroll has not been updated
	update records	the processing of payments and deductions for employees and the recording and saving of them in the program. Once updated, the next payroll can be prepared
	statutory	required by law
	non-statutory	not required by law. Voluntary
	payslip	a form given to each employee detailing their pay and deductions for a given payday

HMRC	Her Majesty's Revenue & Customs. The government department in charge of taxation
P11	a document or record, sometimes referred to as a 'deductions working sheet', where tax and NI values for an employee are recorded for a whole year

Activities

1   Enter year-to-date values in employee records (page 39).

2   Enter payments for the payroll on Friday of Week 9 (6/06/14) (pages 42 and 43).

3   Print (or save) an Update Records Check Report (page 46) and check it against the one on page 46.

4   Print (or save) payslips (page 47). Check those for A Kahn and J Davies against the ones on page 47.

5   Print (or save) payment summaries, parts 1 and 2, and check them against the ones on page 48.

6   Backup and take a screenshot of the backup filename screen (pages 50 and 51).

7   Run (update) the payroll for Friday of Week 9 (6/06/14) (page 51).

5 Entering changes and second payroll

this chapter covers...

Having completed one payroll, we now look at inputting some variations or changes.

This chapter includes how to:

- *add a voluntary deduction from an employee's pay such as a donation to charity*

- *make changes to business and employee details*

- *add a new payment type*

Then we prepare the second payroll and run it for Week 10.

ENTERING CHANGES AND SECOND PAYROLL

Any changes to payroll records and information must be entered into the program as and when they arise. For example:

■ adding voluntary deductions to an employee's record

■ changes or updates to company or business information

■ changes to employee personal details

■ adding new payment types

ENTERING NEW DEDUCTION TYPES

Some deductions like tax, National Insurance and student loan repayments are 'statutory', ie they have to be deducted by law. These deductions are built into the program.

Other deductions may be non-statutory or voluntary, eg private medical insurance, giving to charity, loan repayments. These can be added to the program.

Some voluntary deductions attract tax relief, eg charity donations (also referred to as charitable giving, payroll-giving and Give As You Earn) where the deduction is made before tax is calculated. For example, if gross pay is £400 and £20 of that is deducted as a donation to charity, then tax is due on £380, not on £400.

Case Study

Jay is going to set up two voluntary deductions. She leaves the date as Friday of Week 9 (6 June 2014).

First she sets up donations to an approved charity as a voluntary pay deduction.

She goes to Company/Pay Elements. There are tabs for several other types of adjustments to pay. These include Deductions.

She clicks on the Deductions tab and clicks New. She enters Charity Donation into the description box and places a tick in the PAYE box but leaves other settings as they are.

Now she adds another voluntary deduction – private medical insurance.

She follows the same procedure as for charity donations but this time she does not place a tick in PAYE because there is no tax relief on medical insurance. So she leaves all settings as they are.

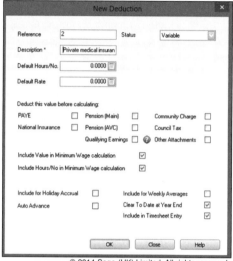

CHANGES TO BUSINESS AND EMPLOYEE DETAILS

You may have to make changes to business information held within the program. For example, bank details may change or be updated, or pension details may alter or be added.

The personal details of employees may alter. For example, a change of home address, or a name change because of marriage.

Case Study

The address for the pension provider, Gennerus Insurance, has been entered wrongly. The address is 71 Thomas Street, Bristol not 17 Thomas Street.

Jay goes to Company/Pension Schemes/Edit scheme 1 (she clicks OK at the warning box)/Provider tab, and changes address details then clicks OK.

Alison Campbell has sent a note saying that her home address has changed. She is now at:

29 Luckwell Drive
St Annes
Bristol
BS4 4TN

Jay opens her employee record and changes her address on the Personal tab. Then she clicks Save.

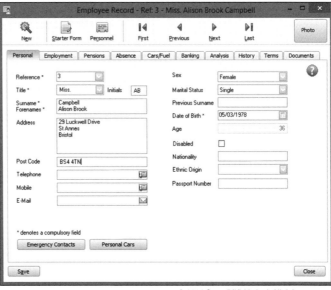

ADDING A NEW PAYMENT TYPE

It may be necessary to add new payment types or rates. For example, bonus or commission payments may be added to basic pay for all or some individuals. Expenses incurred on behalf of the business but paid for personally by employees must be reimbursed to them.

The way these various payment types are set up may differ according to whether they are subject to tax and National Insurance deductions.

- remuneration (pay) is subject to all statutory deductions
- reimbursement is simply a refund of money spent for the business and is therefore not subject to any statutory deductions

Case Study

James Reed is paid commission on a quarterly basis. The next payroll run will include commission of £1,200 due for the quarter ending 31 May.

First Jay needs to set up Commission as a Pay Element. Then she must add this pay element to James Reed's record.

Jay clicks Company/Pay Elements/New. This is pay element number 7. She enters Commission in the Description box but leaves the other boxes as they are, including Variable (as commission may vary each quarter). She clicks OK and then again in the Settings window where she can see Commission has been added as number 7.

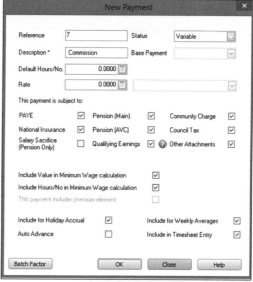

Now she double-clicks on James Reed's record. On the employment tab, she clicks on Pay Elements and adds Pay Element 7 Commission to his record from the drop-down menu. She does not enter any values at this stage.

She saves the new pay element and clicks Save to close James' record.

From time to time Andrew Kahn and James Reed incur travel expenses on behalf of the business. They pay these using their own money so they need to claim them back from the business.

Jay adds another pay element to the program: Expenses. She uses the same procedure she has just used for Commission, but the completion of the record is different.

Although expenses can be paid through the payroll for convenience, they are a refund to the employee of money spent by them for the business, so they are not subject to any deductions of tax or National Insurance. Jay must set up this pay element so that expenses are refunded to the employee in full. She does this by removing all the ticks on the set up screen. She leaves the Default Hours/No. and Rate boxes at zero, and the Status as Variable (because, like commission, expenses are likely to vary).

She clicks OK and OK again to return to the main screen.

Although Jay could add expenses to the records of Andrew and James now, she can also do it when she enters their individual payments for the next payroll run. So she decides to leave it until then.

RUNNING THE PAYROLL – WEEK 10

Once you have made all the changes to the payroll records, you can set about preparing the next payroll run.

Case Study

Having made a few updates, Jay will now run the Week 10 payroll.

The procedure is exactly the same as for the first payroll run. See the panel on the right for a reminder.

She changes the process date to Friday of Week 10 (13/06/14).

Reminder of sequence:
1. Change process date
2. Select employees
3. Enter payments
4. Print pre-update reports
5. Backup
6. Update records

Here are other details that Jay needs:

Timesheet for Week 10:

Employee	Basic	Overtime	Total
G Fleming	35	1	36
A Campbell	35	2	37
J Davies	35	4	39

For each member of staff Jay enters their payments for the week as follows:

Andrew Kahn

Expense payment due of £51.60.

She adds Expenses as a Pay Element using the Add Payment button and inserts 1 in the Hours/No box and £51.60 in the rate box.

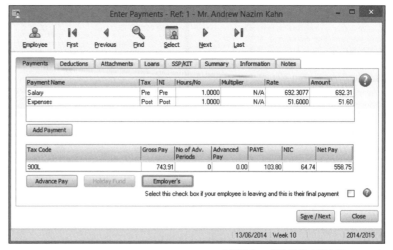

Gemma Fleming

Jay looks at the timesheet and amends the Payments tab to show the correct overtime for the period.

Gemma wants to give £20 to charity each week through the payroll. Jay clicks on her Deductions tab to add her donation.

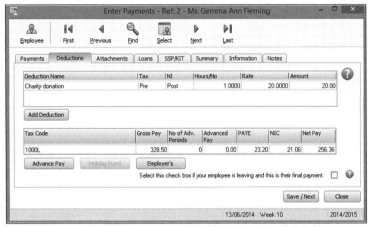

Alison Campbell

Jay looks at the timesheet and amends the Payments tab to show the correct overtime for the period.

James Reed

Commission of £1,200 is due to James Reed. James' payments should already include Commission, so Jay adds the commission value.

An expense payment is due of £74.20. Jay adds Expenses as a payment element and enters the claim using the same process as she did for Andrew Kahn.

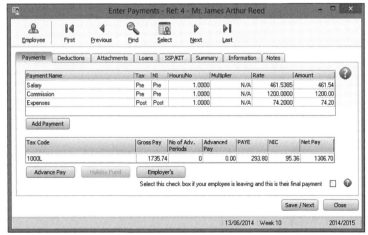

John Davies

Jay looks at the timesheet and amends the Payments tab to show the correct overtime for the period.

Before updating records, Jay takes a look at the Last Updated, Update Status and Last Calculated fields in the on-screen employee list.

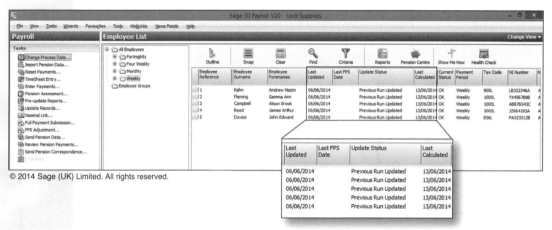

It shows 'Previous Run Updated' for all employees, ie Week 9 payroll was updated. It also shows that calculations have been made for Week 10 (in the Last Calculated column) – the result of Jay entering payments for the current period (but not yet updating them).

Tip – Changing column widths and views

You can change the width of each column by dragging the boundaries. You can also change the view so that the tree or outline does not display in the middle of the screen by clicking Outline on the horizontal toolbar. You can return to the previous view by clicking it again.

Jay clicks on Payroll/Pre-update Reports to preview the Update Records Check Report. This should now be in her Favourites folder.

Date :									**Page :**	1 of 1

Lock Supplies

Update Records Check Report

Tax Month : 3   Week : 10

Ref	Name	Payment Method	Payment Frequency	Tax Code	W1/ M1	NI Cat	Total Gross	Taxable Gross	Tax Paid	Employee NIC	Net Pay
1	AN Kahn	Credit Transfer	Weekly	900L	N	A	743.91	692.31	103.80	64.74	558.75
2	GA Fleming	Credit Transfer	Weekly	1000L	N	A	328.50	308.50	23.20	21.06	256.36
3	AB Campbell	Credit Transfer	Weekly	1000L	N	A	266.00	266.00	14.80	13.62	237.58
4	JA Reed	Credit Transfer	Weekly	1000L	N	A	1,735.74	1,661.54	293.80	95.36	1,306.70
5	JE Davies	Credit Transfer	Weekly	856L	N	A	328.00	328.00	32.80	21.06	274.14
							3,402.15	3,256.35	468.40	215.84	2,633.53

She prints payslips and runs the two payment summary reports as before. These should also be in her Favourites folder.

Here are the payslips for Gemma, showing her charity donation, and for James showing his commission and expenses payments.

Lock Supplies

Department	-					

				Payment Method - Credit Transfer		Payment Period - Weekly	
Office supervisor basic	35.00	9.0000	315.00	PAYE Tax	23.20	Total Gross Pay TD	3325.50
Office supervisor overti	1.00	13.5000	13.50	National Insurance	21.06	Gross for Tax TD	3305.50
				Ee Pension	7.88	Tax paid TD	276.00
				Er Pension	6.57	Earnings For NI TD	3325.00
						National Insurance TD	215.52
						Ee Pension TD	16.74
				Charity donation	20.00	Employers Pension TD	13.95
						Earnings for NI	328.00
						Gross for Tax	308.50
						Total Gross Pay	328.50
						Nat. Insurance No	YX456789B

10	13/06/2014			1000L	2	Ms. GA Fleming	256.36

Lock Supplies

Department	-					

				Payment Method - Credit Transfer		Payment Period - Weekly	
Salary	1.00	461.5385	461.54	PAYE Tax	293.80	Total Gross Pay TD	5889.59
Commission	1.00	1200.0000	1200.00	National Insurance	95.36	Gross for Tax TD	5815.39
Expenses	1.00	74.2000	74.20	Ee Pension	39.88	Tax paid TD	778.00
				Er Pension	33.23	Earnings For NI TD	4958.31
						National Insurance TD	428.58
						Ee Pension TD	50.96
						Employers Pension TD	42.46
						Earnings for NI	805.00
						Gross for Tax	1661.54
						Total Gross Pay	1735.74
						Nat. Insurance No	JZ664192A

10	13/06/2014			1000L	4	Mr. JA Reed	1306.70

Date:					**Lock Supplies**					Page:	1 of 1	
Time:					**Payment Summary (Part 1) Landscape**							

Tax Month : 3   Week : 10   Payment Frequency: Weekly

E'ee Ref	Employee Name	Total Gross	Taxable Gross	Pre-Tax Payment	Pre-Tax Ded'n	Student Loan	PAYE	Employee NIC	Employee Pension*	SSP	SMP	SPP	ASPP	SAP	Post-Tax Payment	Post-Tax Ded'n	B/F	C/F	Net Pay
1	AN Kahn	743.91	692.31	692.31	0.00	0.00	103.80	64.74	16.62	0.00	0.00	0.00	0.00	0.00	51.60	0.00	0.00	0.00	558.75
2	GA Fleming	328.50	308.50	328.50	20.00	0.00	23.20	21.06	7.88	0.00	0.00	0.00	0.00	0.00	0.00	0.00	0.00	0.00	256.36
3	AB Campbell	266.00	266.00	266.00	0.00	0.00	14.80	13.62	0.00	0.00	0.00	0.00	0.00	0.00	0.00	0.00	0.00	0.00	237.58
4	JA Reed	1735.74	1661.54	1661.54	0.00	0.00	293.80	95.36	39.88	0.00	0.00	0.00	0.00	0.00	74.20	0.00	0.00	0.00	1306.70
5	JE Davies	328.00	328.00	328.00	0.00	0.00	32.80	21.06	0.00	0.00	0.00	0.00	0.00	0.00	0.00	0.00	0.00	0.00	274.14
5	Employees	3402.15	3256.35	3276.35	20.00	0.00	468.40	215.84	64.38	0.00	0.00	0.00	0.00	0.00	125.80	0.00	0.00	0.00	2633.53

*Please note this value does not include any contribution made to a salary sacrifice pension scheme.

E'ee Ref	Employee Name	NI'able Earnings	E'ee + E'er NI Contribution	Employer NI Contribution	Employee NI Contribution	Employer NI Rebate	Employee NI Rebate	Employer Pension*	Tax Code	Week 1 / Month 1	NI Cat	Con Out
1	AN Kahn	892.00	139.19	74.45	64.74	0.00	0.00	13.85	900L	N	A	N
2	GA Fleming	328.00	45.28	24.22	21.06	0.00	0.00	6.57	1000L	N	A	N
3	AB Campbell	266.00	29.28	15.66	13.62	0.00	0.00	0.00	1000L	N	A	N
4	JA Reed	805.00	303.47	208.11	95.36	0.00	0.00	33.23	1000L	N	A	N
5	JE Davies	328.00	45.28	24.22	21.06	0.00	0.00	0.00	856L	N	A	N
5	Employees	£2,419.00	£562.50	£346.66	£215.84	£0.00	£0.00	£53.65				

Date:

Time:

Lock Supplies

Payment Summary (Part 2) Landscape

Tax Month : 3   Week : 10   Payment Frequency: Weekly

Page: 1 of 1

Now she updates the records (Payroll/Update Records). She names her own Backup here but Sage will take an automatic backup as part of the updating process. See page 50 for a reminder of the backing up procedure.

Tip – Automatic backup and looking at the backup log

You don't see an automatic backup happen on the screen but you can check that it has happened by going to the File menu (top left of screen) and choosing View Backup & Restore Log. This shows the location and names of the backups and the dates made.

Date :

Time :

Lock Supplies

Backup & Restore Log

Page 1

This report is shown *most recent first*

Backups

Date: 28/07/2014   Company Name: Lock Supplies

Source Dir: (from)   C:\ProgramData\Sage\Payroll\COMPANY_002\PAYDATA\PAYROLL.MDB

Backup File: (to)   C:\ProgramData\Sage\Payroll\COMPANY_002\Archive\W13062014_10-56-06.001

In the main screen Jay can now see the update status is 'Current run updated'.

Employee Reference	Employee Surname	Employee Forenames	Last Updated	Last FPS Date	Update Status	Last Calculated	Current Status	Payment Period	Tax Code	NI Number	N
1	Kahn	Andrew Nazim	13/06/2014		Current Run Updated		OK	Weekly	900L	LB323346A	A
2	Fleming	Gemma Ann	13/06/2014		Current Run Updated		OK	Weekly	1000L	YX456789B	A
3	Campbell	Alison Brook	13/06/2014		Current Run Updated		OK	Weekly	1000L	AB876543C	A
4	Reed	James Arthur	13/06/2014		Current Run Updated		OK	Weekly	1000L	JZ664192A	A
5	Davies	John Edward	13/06/2014		Current Run Updated		OK	Weekly	856L	PA523312B	A

This view provides an easy reference point if she is uncertain about whether she has entered payments or updated records.

Chapter Summary

■ Statutory deductions such as Tax and National Insurance are automatically calculated and deducted when the payroll is run. Pension contributions for members of the pension scheme are automatically deducted. Voluntary deductions such as charity donations can be added to the system.

■ Information about the business may need updating or correcting. For example, changes to bank details or pension provider details must be entered.

■ Employee records must be kept up to date. Any changes such as a change of home address should be entered.

■ There may be new payment types to add to those already in the program. These could include bonuses, commission and expense reimbursement. It is important to get the tax and NI settings right when setting up these payments.

Key Terms

deduction	an amount which is taken off pay. It may be statutory (eg tax and NI) or voluntary (eg pension or charity donation)
commission	pay that is based on a percentage of sales revenue. Usually used to incentivise and reward sales staff
expenses	business expenditure. If paid by an employee, expenses are often refunded through the payroll but free of tax and NI deductions
timesheet	a document recording hours worked and used to calculate pay for hourly paid workers

Activities

1   Set up Charity Donation and Private Medical Insurance as pay deductions (pages 57-58).

2   Amend the address of the pension provider (page 58).

3   Amend Alison Campbell's home address (page 59).

4   Set up Commission as a pay element payment and add it to James Reed's record (page 60).

5   Set up Expenses as a pay element payment (page 61).

6   Enter payments for Week 10 (page 62), remembering to add Expenses to the records of Andrew and James as you go (pages 62-63).

7   Print (or save) an Update Records Check Report (page 64) and check it against the one on page 64.

8   Print (or save) payslips (page 65). Check those for Gemma Fleming and James Reed against the ones on page 65.

9   Print (or save) payment summaries, parts 1 and 2, and check them against the ones on pages 65-66.

10   Run (update) Week 10 payroll, remembering to backup (page 66).

6 More changes and third payroll

this chapter covers...

This chapter expands on the variations to payroll covered in Chapter 5. Here we look at:

- *changing an existing employee's tax code*

- *entering an Attachment of Earnings Order (AEO)*

- *adding a new employee (a 'starter')*

- *advancing pay for a future period*

We also cover what happens when an employee leaves.

We run a third payroll (Week 11) to show how these changes take effect.

Finally we look at how you can delete a payroll for one or more employees and return to an earlier date using Rollback. This is a very useful function if you realise you have made an error after a payroll has been updated.

CHANGING AN EMPLOYEE'S TAX CODE

HMRC will notify you when the tax code of an employee changes.

The tax code is usually made up of a number and a letter. The number multiplied by 10 is the amount of 'free pay' (or untaxed pay) that the employee is entitled to in one year. Any pay over and above this amount is taxed at the basic rate, currently 20%.

In the tax year 2014-15 the personal allowance of free pay is £10,000 so the tax code number is 1000. The £10,000 is divided between the number of paydays, so for monthly pay the tax free allowance is £833 (10,000 divided by 12) and for weekly pay it is £192 (£10,000 divided by 52).

The letter in the tax code shows how the number should be adjusted if the government makes general changes to tax allowances. For example, if the letter is 'L' (as in 1000L) the government may advise that at the start of a new tax year all existing tax codes ending 'L' should have 30 added to the number. This avoids HMRC having to send out millions of new tax code notifications for individual people.

If the number of the tax code changes, it may be because the employee has either paid too much tax or too little tax in the past. It is a way of collecting or refunding back tax.

Normally a tax code is 'cumulative' which means that on each payday the amount of tax due for the year to date is recalculated so that, even if pay varies, the employee's tax for the year is up to date. If the tax code has Week 1/Month 1 after it, then each payday is treated as the first payday of the tax year. This sometimes happens when details about previous employment are missing, or when there has been a gap in someone's employment. It can also be used as a means of collecting or refunding back tax where errors have been made.

Case Study

Before Jay runs the third payroll in Week 11, there are some more amendments and updates to make. She changes the date to Friday of Week 11 (20/06/14), the date of the next payroll run.

HMRC has advised a change of tax code for John Davies effective immediately. It has changed from 856L to 500L Week1/Month 1. Jay updates his record as shown here. She remembers to save the changes.

ENTERING AN ATTACHMENT OF EARNINGS ORDER

A person or an organisation that is owed money by one of your employees can apply to the courts for the debt to be deducted from the employee's pay. A judge may grant an Attachment of Earnings Order (AEO) which is sent to the employer instructing them to take money directly from the employee's pay and send it to the courts until the debt is paid off. Repayment of the debt is usually spread over a period of time.

Examples of where AEOs are issued include for the payment of fines, council tax arrears and child support payments.

There are controls to ensure that an employee still receives enough pay to live on. This amount is called 'protected earnings'. Deductions for AEOs cannot reduce net pay below this amount.

AEOs are statutory deductions, ie the employer is legally bound to deduct the amount of the order from the employee's pay. The different types of order (for example – court fines, child support, council tax arrears) are built into the software so that they are easy to apply.

Case Study

Bristol Courts have sent an Attachment of Earnings Order effective Friday of Week 11 for James Reed for child support payments of £50 per week. The reference is 123456789012.

Jay goes to James Reed's record and clicks Employment/ Pay Elements/ Attachment of Earnings Orders tab. She selects Child Support from the drop-down arrow and enters £50 in the Normal Deduction Rate column and £300 in the Protected Earnings column. The Order Issued Date is Friday of Week 11 (20/06/14) and the reference given above goes in the Order Reference field. There is no Order End date. She clicks Save to exit Pay Elements and Save before closing James' record.

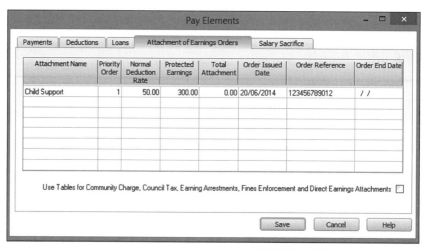

ADDING A NEW EMPLOYEE TO THE PAYROLL

Employees may come and go in business. You need to be able to deal with them joining and leaving.

When a new employee joins, he or she may bring a P45 form with them from their previous employer. This will give personal information and details of their previous employment including pay to date and tax paid. You can use this information to create an employee record in the payroll program.

If the new employee does not have a P45 – perhaps because they have not worked before, or have been out of work for some time – you will get them to complete a starter declaration. You can use a form issued by HMRC called a 'Starter checklist'. On this, they must opt for one of three statements (A, B or C) which will point you, as the employer, to the tax code to use for the employee.

As with existing members of staff, you must include certain minimum information by law in the new employee record. See page 23.

Case Study

A new member of staff started on Monday of Week 11. His details are as follows:

EMPLOYEE RECORD CARD			
Reference	6	Date of Birth	24/03/86
Works Number	Not used	Employee Start Date	16 June 2014
Title	Mr		(Monday of Week 11)
Surname	Abbiati	Payment Method	Credit transfer
Forenames	Giovanni Dino	Payment Frequency	Weekly
Address	16 Devizes Road Bradford on Avon Wiltshire	Employee provided form	P45 (below)
		Starting declaration	None
		Pension Scheme	1 Main scheme
Postcode	BA15 1SE	Job title	Accounts Technician
Sex	Male	Gross salary	£23,000 per year

EMPLOYEE P45			
Previous employment tax ref:	123/CD789	Tax code:	1000L
Date left previous employment:	30 May 2014	NI number:	KR 654321 C
Pay to date:	£3,000	NI category:	A
Tax paid:	£266.60	Continue student loan deductions:	Yes

Jay goes to Employee/Quick employee and adds Giovanni's details to the program.

Quick Employee Ref: 6 - Basic Details				×

Reference *	6	Works No.	6	Employee provided form	P45
Title *	Mr.			Starting Declaration *	None
Surname *	Abbiati			Previous Employment Tax Dist./Ref.	123 / CD789
Forenames *	Giovanni Dino			Date Left Previous Employment	30/05/2014
Address	16 Devizes Road Bradford on Avon Wiltshire			Total Pay to Date	3000.00
				Total Tax to Date	266.60
Post Code	BA15 1SE			Tax Code at Leaving Date *	1000L Week 1/Month 1 ☐
Home Tel.				N.I. Number *	☐ Not Known
Mobile Tel.					KR 654321 C
Marital Status	Single Sex Male			N.I. Category *	A - Standard Rate Contributions
Date of Birth *	24/03/1986			Continue Student Loan deductions?	Yes
Passport Number				Pension	1 - Main scheme
RTI Payroll ID	21B651415236A0B2 Edit			Department	No Department
				Job Title	Accounts Technician
Start Date *	16/06/2014			Apply Minimum Wage check ☐	Apprentice Rate ☐
Welfare to Work	☐				
Payment Method	Credit Transfer			Gross Salary	23000.0000 per Year
Payment Frequency	Weekly				
Sort Code	00-00-00 A/C No.				
A/C Name					
BACS Ref.					
A/C Type	Bank Account				
Roll Number					

Payment Name	Hours/No.	Rate

Deduction Name	Hours/No.	Rate

* denotes a compulsory field

Save & Clear   Save & Retain   Help   Close

ADVANCING PAY

If an employee takes a holiday (sometimes referred to as 'leave') the employer may want to pay them in advance for the period they are away.

On the last payday before the employee goes on holiday, you can instruct the payroll program to calculate advanced pay in addition to their normal pay. You can advance pay that is just basic pay or it can include additional items such as bonuses, expense payments and voluntary deductions. Tax and NI will be automatically calculated for the advanced period.

When the next payday arrives, for which the employee has received advanced pay, the program will not allow any more pay to be processed for that employee.

PREPARING FOR AN EMPLOYEE TO LEAVE

If an employee has given notice that they will be leaving, you need to decide the date of the employee's final pay. When you process this (and you need to make sure they receive all they are entitled to) you tell the program that the employee is leaving before you update the records.

After you have updated the records you will be able to process the leaver's P45. See page 80.

Case Study

Now Jay can run the payroll for Week 11 following the sequence shown on the right.

The process date is Friday of Week 11 (20/06/14).

Reminder of sequence:
1. Change process date
2. Select employees
3. Enter payments
4. Print pre-update reports
5. Backup
6. Update records

Timesheet for hourly paid staff.

Employee	Basic	Overtime	Total
G Fleming	35	2	37
A Campbell	35	1	36
J Davies	35	5	40

A Kahn

This week Andrew is just getting his weekly pay. There is no expense payment so Jay ensures that on the line for expenses she changes the number to '0'. If she does this, she doesn't need to amend the Rate.

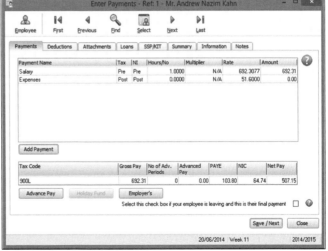

G Fleming

Jay enters Gemma's hours for the current period from the timesheet. Her charity donation will be deducted automatically.

Gemma is taking a week's holiday starting Monday of Week 12 (23/06/14). She will receive one week's advanced pay. To set this up, Jay clicks on the Advance Pay button. She must enter exactly what is to be paid and deducted (non-statutory deductions) in advance.

She enters 1 period to advance, then enters just Gemma's 35 hours basic pay.

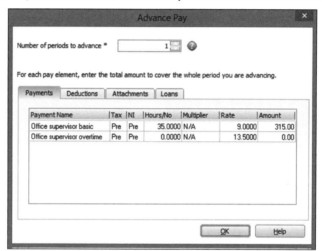

Gemma's charity donation is to be suspended for her holiday week so on the Deductions tab she makes sure that all values are zero.

Once the advanced pay has been added, Gemma's Enter Payments screen looks like this.

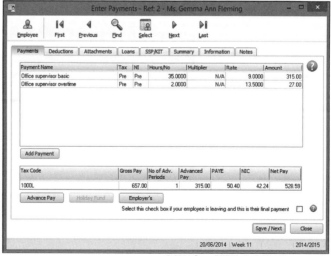

A Campbell

Alison's hours are entered from the timesheet.

She is leaving today (Friday of Week 11). Jay clicks the check box at the bottom right of the screen to indicate this is her final pay.

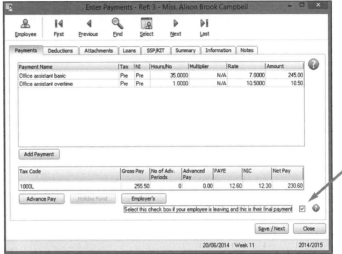

J Reed

James will receive only his basic pay this week so Jay enters '0' against his expenses element and his commission element.

His Attachment of Earnings Order (AEO) will be deducted automatically. Jay can check this by looking at James' summary tab.

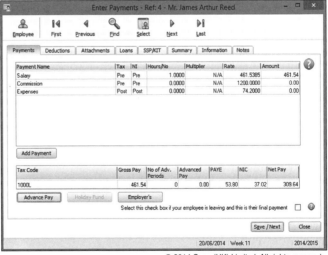

J Davies

John's hours are entered from the timesheet.

G Abbiati

Giovanni's pay and deductions (including his student loan repayment) will be calculated automatically from the entries made when he joined the payroll.

Note that he is due a small tax refund this week.

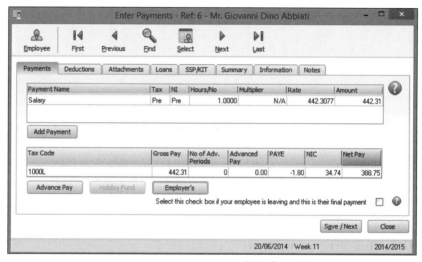

Tip – Tax refunds

In some circumstances the program may calculate a tax refund for the employee. The refund is added to the pay. This might happen when a new member of staff joins or when an employee's tax code changes.

Now Jay has entered the payroll for Week 11, she previews and checks the Update Records Check Report.

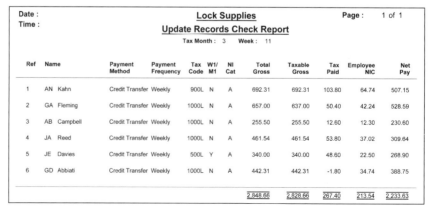

Date :							Lock Supplies		Page :	1 of 1
Time :							Update Records Check Report			
							Tax Month : 3 Week : 11			

Ref	Name	Payment Method	Payment Frequency	Tax Code	W1/ M1	NI Cat	Total Gross	Taxable Gross	Tax Paid	Employee NIC	Net Pay
1	AN Kahn	Credit Transfer	Weekly	900L	N	A	692.31	692.31	103.80	64.74	507.15
2	GA Fleming	Credit Transfer	Weekly	1000L	N	A	657.00	637.00	50.40	42.24	528.59
3	AB Campbell	Credit Transfer	Weekly	1000L	N	A	255.50	255.50	12.60	12.30	230.60
4	JA Reed	Credit Transfer	Weekly	1000L	N	A	461.54	461.54	53.80	37.02	309.64
5	JE Davies	Credit Transfer	Weekly	500L	Y	A	340.00	340.00	48.60	22.50	268.90
6	GD Abbiati	Credit Transfer	Weekly	1000L	N	A	442.31	442.31	-1.80	34.74	388.75
							2,848.66	2,828.66	267.40	213.54	2,233.63

She runs payslips and payment summaries for tax and NI at this point. Here is Gemma's payslip showing the advanced pay for her holiday.

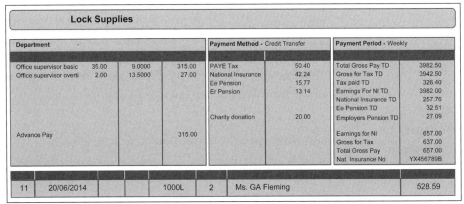

Lock Supplies						
Department	-			**Payment Method** - Credit Transfer		**Payment Period** - Weekly

Office supervisor basic	35.00	9.0000	315.00
Office supervisor overti	2.00	13.5000	27.00

PAYE Tax	50.40
National Insurance	42.24
Ee Pension	15.77
Er Pension	13.14
Charity donation	20.00

Total Gross Pay TD	3982.50
Gross for Tax TD	3942.50
Tax paid TD	326.40
Earnings For NI TD	3982.00
National Insurance TD	257.76
Ee Pension TD	32.51
Employers Pension TD	27.09

Advance Pay	315.00

Earnings for NI	657.00
Gross for Tax	637.00
Total Gross Pay	657.00
Nat. Insurance No	YX456789B

| 11 | 20/06/2014 | | | 1000L | 2 | Ms. GA Fleming | 528.59 |

Lock Supplies

Date:

Time:

Page: 1 of 1

Payment Summary (Part 1) Landscape

Tax Month : 3   Week : 11   Payment Frequency: Weekly

E'ee Ref	Employee Name	Total Gross	Taxable Gross	Pre-Tax Payment	Pre-Tax Ded'n	Student Loan	PAYE	Employee NIC	Employee Pension*	SSP	SMP	SPP	ASPP	SAP	Post-Tax Payment	Post-Tax Ded'n	B/F	C/F	Net Pay
1	AN Kahn	692.31	692.31	692.31	0.00	0.00	103.80	64.74	16.62	0.00	0.00	0.00	0.00	0.00	0.00	0.00	0.00	0.00	507.15
2	GA Fleming	657.00	637.00	657.00	20.00	0.00	50.40	42.24	15.77	0.00	0.00	0.00	0.00	0.00	0.00	0.00	0.00	0.00	528.59
3	AB Campbell	255.50	255.50	255.50	0.00	0.00	12.60	12.30	0.00	0.00	0.00	0.00	0.00	0.00	0.00	0.00	0.00	0.00	230.60
4	JA Reed	461.54	461.54	461.54	0.00	0.00	53.80	37.02	11.08	0.00	0.00	0.00	0.00	0.00	0.00	50.00	0.00	0.00	309.64
5	JE Davies	340.00	340.00	340.00	0.00	0.00	48.60	22.50	0.00	0.00	0.00	0.00	0.00	0.00	0.00	0.00	0.00	0.00	268.90
6	GD Abbiati	442.31	442.31	442.31	0.00	10.00	-1.80	34.74	10.62	0.00	0.00	0.00	0.00	0.00	0.00	0.00	0.00	0.00	388.75
6	Employees	2848.66	2828.66	2848.66	20.00	10.00	267.40	213.54	54.09	0.00	0.00	0.00	0.00	0.00	0.00	50.00	0.00	0.00	2233.63

Lock Supplies

Date:

Time:

Page: 1 of 1

Payment Summary (Part 2) Landscape

Tax Month : 3   Week : 11   Payment Frequency: Weekly

E'ee Ref	Employee Name	NI'able Earnings	E'ee + E'er NI Contribution	Employer NI Contribution	Employee NI Contribution	Employer NI Rebate	Employee NI Rebate	Employer Pension*	Tax Code	Week 1 / Month 1	NI Cat	Con Out
1	AN Kahn	692.00	139.19	74.45	64.74	0.00	0.00	13.85	900L	N	A	N
2	GA Fleming	657.00	90.81	48.57	42.24	0.00	0.00	13.14	1000L	N	A	N
3	AB Campbell	255.00	26.44	14.14	12.30	0.00	0.00	0.00	1000L	N	A	N
4	JA Reed	461.00	79.59	42.57	37.02	0.00	0.00	9.23	1000L	N	A	N
5	JE Davies	340.00	48.37	25.87	22.50	0.00	0.00	0.00	500L	Y	A	N
6	GD Abbiati	442.00	74.69	39.95	34.74	0.00	0.00	8.85	1000L	N	A	N
6	Employees	£2,847.00	£459.09	£245.55	£213.54	£0.00	£0.00	£45.07				

Once she is happy with the reports, she Updates the records, remembering to backup with her own filename as she goes.

Jay notices that the screen shows 'later run updated' for Gemma because she has received a week's advanced pay for her holiday period.

Outline	Swap	Clear	Find	Criteria	Reports	Pension Centre	Show Me How	Health Check

Employee Reference	Employee Surname	Employee Forenames	Last Updated	Last FPS Date	Update Status	Last Calculated	Current Status	Payment Period	Tax Code	NI Number	N
1	Kahn	Andrew Nazim	20/06/2014		Current Run Updated		OK	Weekly	900L	LB322346A	A
2	Fleming	Gemma Ann	27/06/2014		Later Run Updated		Holiday	Weekly	1000L	YX456789B	A
3	Campbell	Alison Brook	20/06/2014		Current Run Updated		OK	Weekly	1000L	AB876543C	A

LEAVER DOCUMENTATION

When an employee leaves the business you must issue a P45 form. You have already seen how a P45 is used to input details when a new employee joins the business; you must also provide your leaver with the same information. It is important for his/her next employment. HMRC is also informed through RTI submission as part of the leaving process.

Case Study

Jay must now deal with Alison's leaving documentation.

She goes into her record and clicks on the employment tab. She clicks the Leaver button. The Leaver Wizard appears.

She works through the wizard entering a leaving date of Friday of Week 11 (20/06/14).

She prints the P11 details reports for NIC (National Insurance Contributions) and PAYE (tax) by using the drop-down arrow.

Date :												Page :
Time :				**Lock Supplies**								
				P11 Deduction Card (PAYE Details)								
				Year To 5th April 2015								

Employer Name:	Lock Supplies		Reference:	3		Surname:	Campbell		Forename(s):	Alison Brook
Tax Ref / Dist:	034 / S650		NI No. :	AB876543C		D.O.B. :	05/03/1988		Works No. :	
Payment Type:	Credit Transfer		Start Date:	01/10/2011		Leaving Date:	20/06/2014			
Payment Period:	Weekly									

	Tax Code:	Current	Prev-1	Prev-2	Prev-3	Prev-4
Student Loan Case: N		1000L	1000L			
	Mth/Wk Applied:		9			

Wk / Mth No	Pay in theweek or month including Statutory Payments (SSP/ SMP/SPP/ASPP/SAP)	Total pay to date	Total free pay to date	(K-Codes only) Total 'additional pay' to date (Table A)	Total taxable pay to date i.e column 3 minus column 4a, OR column 3 plus column 4b	Total tax due to date as shown by Taxable Pay Tables	******* (K-Codes) ****** Tax Due at end of current period R = refund	Regulatory Limit i.e 50% of column 2	Tax deducted or refunded in the week or month R= refund	(K-Codes) Tax not deducted owing to the regulatory limit
	(2) £ p	(3) £ p	(4a) £ p	(4b) £ p	(5) £ p	(6) £ p	(6a) £ p	(6b) £ p	(7) £ p	(8) £ p
B/F	2023.00	0.00	0.00	0.00	0.00	0.00	0.00	0.00	96.00	0.00
9	245.00	2268.00	1732.41	0.00	535.59	107.00	0.00	0.00	11.00	0.00
10	266.00	2534.00	1924.90	0.00	609.10	121.80	0.00	0.00	14.80	0.00
11	255.50	2789.50	2117.39	0.00	672.11	134.40	0.00	0.00	12.60	0.00
		0.00	<- Previous Employment ->			0.00	Widows & Orphans Contributions			
		2789.50	<- This Employment ->			134.40				
		2789.50	<- Total To Date ->			134.40	0.00			

Date :
Time :

Page : 1 of 1

Lock Supplies
P11 Deduction Card (NIC Details)
Year To 5th April 2015

Employer Name:	Lock Supplies	Reference: 3	Surname: Campbell	Forename(s): Alison Brook
Tax Ref / Dist:	034 / S650		N.I. No.: AB876543C	D.O.B.: 05/03/1988
Payment Type:	Credit Transfer			Works No.:
Payment Period:	Weekly			Start Date: 01/10/2011
Student Loan Case:	N			Leaving Date: 20/06/2014

*********** National Insurance (n.b. LEL = Lower Earnings Limit, PT = Primary Threshold, UAP = Upper Accrual Point, UEL = Upper Earnings Limit) ************

Earnings at the LEL (where earnings reach or exceed the LEL) £	Earnings above the LEL, up to and including the PT £	Earnings above the PT, up to and including the UAP £	Earnings above the UAP, and including the UEL £	Total of employee's & employer's contributions mark minus amounts 'R' £ p	Employee's contributions due on all earnings above the PT £ p	Statutory Sick Pay paid to employee in the week or month included in column 2 £ p	Statutory Maternity Pay paid to employee in the week or month included in column 2 £ p	Statutory Paternity Pay paid to employee in the week or month included in column 2 £ p	Additional Statutory Paternity Pay paid to employee in the week or month included in column 2 £ p	Statutory Adoption Pay paid to employee in the week or month included in column 2 £ p	Student Loan Deductions £	Wk / Mth No
(1a)	(1b)	(1c)	(1d)	(1e)	(1f)	(1g)	(1h)	(1i)	(1j)	(1k)	(1l)	
888.00	336.00	799.00	0.00	206.14	95.88	0.00	0.00	0.00	0.00	0.00	0	B/F
111.00	42.00	92.00	0.00	23.86	11.10	0.00	0.00	0.00	0.00	0.00	0	9
111.00	42.00	113.00	0.00	29.28	13.62	0.00	0.00	0.00	0.00	0.00	0	10
111.00	42.00	102.00	0.00	26.44	12.30	0.00	0.00	0.00	0.00	0.00	0	11
1221.00	462.00	1106.00	0.00	285.72	132.90	0.00	0.00	0.00	0.00	0.00	0	
1a 1,221.00	1b 462.00	1c 1,106.00	1d 0.00	1e 285.72	1f 132.90							

NI CAT A

SCON Ref :

Before clicking Finish, she prints all three pages of the P45 Plain Paper (for eSubmissions). These are shown over the next 3 pages of the text.

	P45 Part 1A
HM Revenue & Customs	**Details of employee leaving work**
	Copy for employee

1 Employer PAYE reference	5 Student Loan deductions
Office number Reference number	☐ Student Loan deductions to continue
034 / S650	6 Tax Code at leaving date
2 Employee's National Insurance number	1000L
AB 87 65 43 C	If week 1 or month 1 applies, enter 'X' in the box below.
3 Title - enter MR, MRS, MISS, MS or other title	Week 1/Month 1 ☐
Miss.	7 Last entries on P11 *Deductions Working Sheet*. **Complete only if Tax Code is cumulative** If there is an 'X' at box 6 there will be no entries here.
Surname or family name	
Campbell	Week number 11 Month number ☐
First or given name(s)	Total pay to date
Alison Brook	£ 2789.50 p
4 Leaving date *DD MM YYYY*	Total tax to date
20 06 2014	£ 134.40 p

8 This employment pay and tax. If no entry here, the amounts are those shown at box 7.	12 Employee's private address
Total pay in this employment	29 Luckwell Drive St Annes Bristol
£ p	
Total tax in this employment	Postcode
£ p	BS4 4TN
9 Works number/Payroll number and Department or branch (if any)	13 I certify that the details entered in items 1 to 11 on this form are correct.
	Employer name and address
	Lock Supplies Unit 43 Westdown Industrial Estate Bristol Road Bath
10 Gender. Enter 'X' in the appropriate box	
Male ☐ Female ☒	Postcode
11 Date of birth *DD MM YYYY*	BA1 7QJ
05 03 1988	Date *DD MM YYYY*

To the employee

The P45 is in three parts. Please keep this part (Part1A) safe. Copies are not available. You might need the information in Part 1A to fill in a Tax Return if you are sent one.

Please read the notes in Part 2 that accompany Part 1A. The notes give some important information about what you should do next and what you should do with Parts 2 and 3 of this form.

Tax Credits

Tax credits are flexible. They adapt to changes in your life, such as leaving a job. If you need to let us know about a change in your income, phone **0845 300 3900**.

To the new employer

If your new employee gives you this Part 1A, please return it to them. Deal with Parts 2 and 3 as normal.

P45(Online) Part 1 A

HMRC 10/08

HM Revenue & Customs

P45 Part 2
Details of employee leaving work
Copy for new employer

---

1 Employer PAYE reference

Office number   Reference number

034 / S650

2 Employee's National Insurance number

AB 87 65 43 C

3 Title - enter MR, MRS, MISS, MS or other title

Miss.

Surname or family name

Campbell

First or given name(s)

Alison Brook

4 Leaving date *DD MM YYYY*

2 0   0 6   2 0 1 4

5 Student Loan deductions

Student Loan deductions to continue

6 Tax Code at leaving date

1000L

If week 1 or month 1 applies, enter 'X' in the box below.

Week 1/Month 1

7 Last entries on P11 *Deductions Working Sheet.*
Complete only if Tax Code is cumulative. If there is an 'X' at box 6 there will be no entries here.

Week number   11   Month number

Total pay to date

£   2789.50   p

Total tax to date

£   134.40   p

To the employee
This form is important to you. Take good care of it and keep it safe. Copies are not available. Please keep Parts 2 and 3 of the form together and do not alter them in any way.

Going to a new job
Give Parts 2 and 3 of this form to your new employer, or you will have tax deducted using the emergency code and may pay too much tax. If you do not want your new employer to know the details on this form, send it to your HM Revenue & Customs (HMRC) office immediately with a letter saying so and giving the name and address of your new employer. HMRC can make special arrangements, but you may pay too much tax for a while as a result of this.

Going abroad
If you are going abroad or returning to a country outside the UK ask for form P85 *Leaving the United Kingdom* from any HMRC office or Enquiry Centre.

Becoming self-employed
You must register with HMRC within three months of becoming self-employed or you could incur a penalty. To register as newly self-employed see The Phone Book under HM Revenue & Customs or go to **www.hmrc.gov.uk** to get a copy of the booklet SE1 *Are you thinking of working for yourself?*

Claiming Jobseeker's Allowance or Employment and Support Allowance (ESA)
Take this form to your Jobcentre Plus Office. They will pay you any tax refund you may be entitled to when your claim ends, or at 5 April if this is earlier.

Not working and claiming Jobseeker's Allowance or Employment and Support Allowance (ESA)
If you have paid tax and wish to claim a refund ask for form P50 *Claiming tax back when you have stopped working* from any HMRC office or Enquiry Centre.

Help
If you need further help you can contact any HMRC office or Enquiry Centre. You can find us in The Phone Book under HM Revenue & Customs or go to **www.hmrc.gov.uk**

To the new employer
Check this form and complete boxes 8 to 18 in Part 3 and prepare a form P11 *Deductions Working Sheet.* Follow the instructions in the Employer Helpbook *E13 Day-to-day payroll,* for how to prepare a P11 *Deductions Working Sheet.* Send Part 3 of this form to your HMRC office immediately. Keep Part 2.

P45(Online) Part 2   HMRC 10/08

HM Revenue & Customs

P45 Part 3
New employee details
For completion by new employer

File your employee's P45 online at **www.hmrc.gov.uk**

Use capital letters when completing this form

1 Employer PAYE reference

Office number   Reference number

034 / S650

2 Employee's National Insurance number

AB 87 65 43 C

3 Title - enter MR, MRS, MISS, MS or other title

Miss.

Surname or family name

Campbell

First or given name(s)

Alison Brook

4 Leaving date *DD MM YYYY*

20 06 2014

5 Student Loan deductions

☐ Student Loan deductions to continue

6 Tax Code at leaving date

1000L

If week 1 or month 1 applies, enter 'X' in the box below.

Week 1/Month 1 ☐

7 Last entries on P11 *Deductions Working Sheet*.
Complete only if Tax Code is cumulative. If there is an 'X' at box 6 there will be no entries here.

Week number 11   Month number ☐

Total pay to date

£ 2789.50 p

Total tax to date

£ 134.40 p

To the new employer Complete boxes 8 to 18 and send P45 Part 3 only to your HMRC office immediately.

8 New Employer PAYE reference

Office number   Reference number

☐ / ☐

9 Date new employment started *DD MM YYYY*

☐ ☐ ☐

10 Works number/Payroll number and Department or branch (if any)

☐

11 Enter 'P' here if employee will not be paid by you between the date employment began and the next 5 April. ☐

12 Enter Tax Code in use if different to the Tax Code at box 6.

☐

If week 1 or month 1 applies, enter 'X' in the box below.

Week 1/Month 1 ☐

13 If the tax figure you are entering on P11 *Deductions Working Sheet* differs from box 7 (see the E13 *Employer Helpbook Day-to-day payroll*) please enter the figure here.

£ ☐ p

14 New employee's job title or job description

☐

15 Employee's private address

☐

Postcode

☐

16 Gender. Enter 'X' in the appropriate box

Male ☐   Female ☐

17 Date of birth *DD MM YYYY*

☐ ☐ ☐

Declaration

18 I have prepared a P11 *Deductions Working Sheet* in accordance with the details above.

Employer name and address

☐

Postcode

☐

Date *DD MM YYYY*

☐ ☐ ☐

P45(Online) Part 3

HMRC 10/08

Now she completes the wizard by clicking Finish and saves and closes Alison's record. Notice that her Status on the main employee list is now 'Leaver'.

> **Tip – Changing list order**
>
> You can change the order of the employee list by clicking on the column heading, eg Employee Reference. If you click on the heading you will see an arrow. Click on the arrow to sort the data in ascending or descending order. If you right click on the heading you will see some more choices regarding the appearance of the list. Play around with these options for a moment and try sorting by surname (alphabetical) or adding colours to the columns.

ROLLBACK

If you find you have run a whole payroll and it includes an error for only one or some of the employees, you have two choices:

1 Restore the backup taken before the payroll run, amend the payroll and run it again for all employees.

2 Use 'rollback'. Rollback allows you to delete payroll runs for any or all of your employees and process their payments again. For example, suppose that you had entered salary or pay wrongly when setting up pay for an employee, and then you had run the whole payroll without realising that the pay amount was wrong. By using rollback, you could re-run that employee's pay for the period while leaving all other employees unchanged.

Case Study

Giovanni's salary was wrongly entered when Jay set up his pay. It should have been £25,000 per annum (not £23,000).

Jay will use rollback to re-run Giovanni's pay for Week 11 so she selects just Giovanni Abbiati's record on the screen. She does not open the record.

She then clicks Wizards on the Menu bar and chooses the Rollback option. The Rollback Wizard appears.

She takes a backup then proceeds through the wizard.

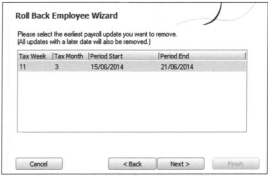

Jay sees a warning on the screen at the end of the wizard, stating that the pay date selected (the only one there) is the oldest and asking if she wants to clear other information relating to Giovanni's set up. She is careful to click **No** here.

She clicks OK when another warning comes up about pension status.

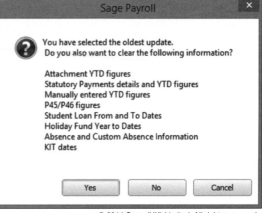

Now Jay amends Giovanni's pay by changing his salary to £25,000 per year on the Employment tab of his employment record.

She now enters his pay for Week 11 again in the normal way but ensures that only his record is selected.

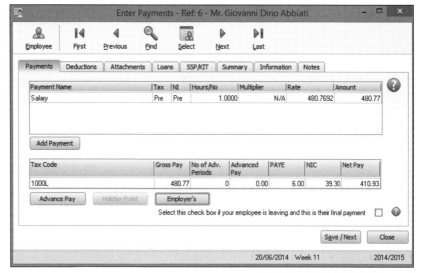

Jay runs a pre-update report and payslip (not shown) just for Giovanni.

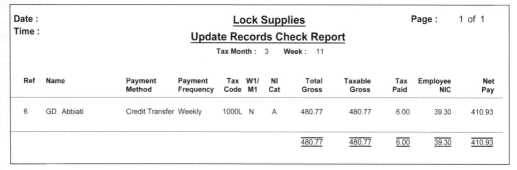

Date :			Lock Supplies						Page :	1 of 1	
Time :			Update Records Check Report								
			Tax Month : 3	Week : 11							
Ref	Name	Payment Method	Payment Frequency	Tax Code	W1/ M1	NI Cat	Total Gross	Taxable Gross	Tax Paid	Employee NIC	Net Pay
6	GD Abbiati	Credit Transfer	Weekly	1000L	N	A	480.77	480.77	6.00	39.30	410.93
							480.77	480.77	6.00	39.30	410.93

Finally, Jay updates the record of Giovanni only.

■ The amount of tax an employee pays is dependent upon their tax code. The tax code is issued by HMRC. From time to time HMRC may advise a change to the tax code of an existing employee. This must be input in the employee record.

■ In addition to statutory deductions such as tax, National Insurance and student loan repayments, an employer may have to implement court orders to take money from an employees' pay. These are called Attachment of Earnings Orders and include orders for council tax arrears and child support payments. The amount deducted must be sent by the business to the agency in charge of collecting the debt.

■ If a new employee ('starter') joins the business, a record must be set up for him or her. As with existing employees, the record will include important personal and job information, as well as details of previous employment. This is often given on a P45 form, completed by a former employer, which the new employee will hand to you.

■ Employers may wish to pay their staff in advance for periods of absence such as holidays. On the payday before the period of absence, the employee will receive additional pay for when he/she is away. This includes the usual statutory deductions.

■ If an employee leaves the business a P45 form must be generated for the leaver to take with them. It includes details of gross pay and tax deducted in the tax year up to the date of leaving. The information is also reported to HMRC via RTI.

■ If you need to re-run a payroll for any employee/s you can select them and use 'rollback'. This deletes the specified payroll (or payrolls) and returns you to the date from which you can re-process just that employee's pay without affecting any others.

Key Terms

AEO	Attachment of Earnings Order. A court order for the employer to deduct money from an employee's pay and send it to the court
starter	an employee who joins a business
leaver	an employee who leaves a business
P45	a form issued to an employee when he/she leaves, giving details of the employment including tax paid to date and tax code. The information on the form is used by a new employer to set up a new employee record, and by HMRC to record changes in employment

personal allowance an amount of free or untaxed pay that every worker is entitled to. Set by the government each year

rollback the option to go back to a previous point or date and run the payroll again for one or more employees

advanced pay pay that relates to a future period but is paid now. Often used when staff go on holiday to provide them with pay when they are away

Activities

1   Change John Davies' tax code to 500L Week1/Month1 (page 71).

2   Enter an AEO on James Reed's record (page 72).

3   Add Giovanni Abbiati to the payroll. Enter his salary as £23,000 per year (pages 73-74).

4   Enter payments for Week 11 payroll including:

   a.   Enter one week's advanced pay for Gemma's holiday (page 76).

   b.   Enter Alison Campbell as a leaver on 20 June (page 77).

5   Print (or save) an Update Records Check Report (page 78) and check it against the one on page 78.

6   Print (or save) payslips (page 79). Check Gemma Fleming's payslip against the one on page 79.

7   Print (or save) payment summaries, parts 1 and 2, and check them against the ones on page 79.

8   Update the payroll and then print (or save) Alison's P45, P11 Deduction Card (PAYE details) and P11 Deduction Card (NIC details) (pages 80-81). Check the P45 against the one on pages 82-84.

9   Rollback Giovanni's pay for Week 11. Amend his annual salary from £23,000 to £25,000 and then print (or save) an Update Records Check Report for him only. Check it against the one on page 87. Now re-run Week 11 payroll just for Giovanni.

7 Further changes and fourth payroll

this chapter covers...

In this final chapter, we cover how to enter a net payment for an employee: you input what the net pay is to be and the software works out the statutory deductions to arrive at gross pay.

We also look at how to amend pay rates for individual employees.

Finally we run a fourth payroll (Week 12) and look at producing period end reports.

ADDING A PAYMENT NET OF TAX

If you want to ensure that an employee receives a specific amount of net pay, you can enter a net pay addition. The program will 'gross up' the amount so that the correct amount of tax and National Insurance is added.

For example, if an employee's gross pay is normally £400 and you want him to receive an additional net pay bonus of £50, then the software will calculate the gross pay that would result. The gross pay with the bonus will be more than £50 higher than the gross pay without the bonus. See the example below.

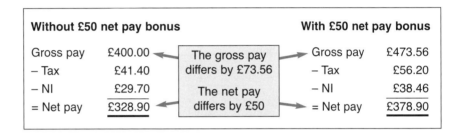

Without £50 net pay bonus			**With £50 net pay bonus**	
Gross pay	£400.00	The gross pay differs by £73.56	Gross pay	£473.56
– Tax	£41.40		– Tax	£56.20
– NI	£29.70	The net pay differs by £50	– NI	£38.46
= Net pay	£328.90		= Net pay	£378.90

Case Study

Jay changes the date to Friday of Week 12 (27/06/14).

Each member of staff who was working for the business on 1 April 2014 has been awarded a bonus of £50 which is to be paid net of any tax and National Insurance in Week 12's payroll.

First Jay needs to set up a new Pay Element called Bonus but unlike the other payments she has entered, she must use the Net Payments tab. So she clicks Company/Pay Elements/Net Payments/New.

This is payment reference 9. Jay enters Bonus in Description, 1 in Hours/No and 50.00 in Rate and Fixed in Status.

She checks Employee's Tax and NI in the Payment Adjusted For fields and leaves all other fields as they are.

She clicks OK.

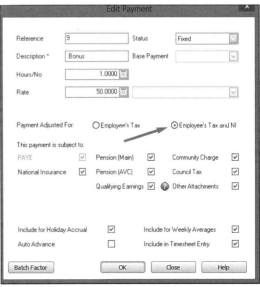

AMENDING PAY RATES

From time to time it may be necessary to change the pay rates of employees, perhaps because of promotion or increased responsibility. Although it is possible to make changes at a company-wide level where several employees receive the same rate, such a change is beyond the scope of this Unit. The Case Study shows how to amend individual pay rates within an employee record.

Case Study

An increase in hourly pay has been agreed for John Davies, effective immediately, as follows:

Basic rate £ per hour	Overtime rate £ per hour
8.40	12.60

Jay goes to John's employee record, clicks on the Employment tab and Pay Elements. She changes the hourly rates in the Rate field and clicks Save and Close.

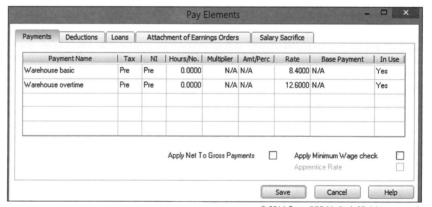

RUNNING THE PAYROLL – WEEK 12

You can now run your fourth payroll. Once you have done this you will have a fairly complete picture of computerised payroll: you will have met and dealt with almost all possible eventualities that might occur in straightforward, day-to-day payroll.

Case Study

Now Jay can run Week 12 payroll.

She checks the process date is 27/06/14 (Friday of Week 12) and follows the sequence on the right again.

Reminder of sequence:
1. Change process date
2. Select employees
3. Enter payments
4. Print pre-update reports
5. Backup
6. Update records

Here is the timesheet for hourly paid staff. It is only for John Davies, as Gemma is on holiday and Alison has left.

Employee	Basic	Overtime	Total
J Davies	35	3	38

When Jay selects all employees and Enter Payments, a warning appears telling her that something is wrong:

She needs to deselect both Gemma (because she has received advanced pay for Week 12 in the last payroll run), and Alison (because she has left). She can either let the program do this by clicking Yes, or she can click No but deselect them herself.

Tip – Excluding leavers from the list

If you do not want leavers' details to appear on the list, you can click on Criteria and check the box that says Exclude Current Year Leavers.

A Kahn

Andrew is to receive his normal salary plus the net pay bonus of £50. There are no expenses.

Jay clicks Add payment in his Payments tab and adds Bonus.

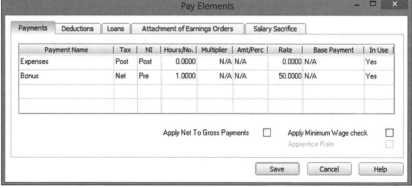

G Fleming

There are no entries for Gemma in Week 12 because she is on holiday and she received advanced pay last week. Gemma will receive her bonus in her next pay.

J Reed

James receives his normal salary. No expenses, no commission.

Jay adds his net pay bonus of £50, as for Andrew.

J Davies

John's hours are entered from the timesheet. He will receive his new hourly rates.

Jay adds his net pay bonus of £50 as for other staff.

G Abbiati

Giovanni does not receive a Bonus as he was not working for the business on 1 April, so he just receives his salary which will be calculated automatically. It should be correct this time!

Jay runs the Pre-update reports for Week 12 and checks them.

Date : Time :			Lock Supplies Update Records Check Report Tax Month : 3 Week : 12									Page : 1 of 1
Ref	Name		Payment Method	Payment Frequency	Tax Code	W1/ M1	NI Cat	Total Gross	Taxable Gross	Tax Paid	Employee NIC	Net Pay
1	AN	Kahn	Credit Transfer	Weekly	900L	N	A	765.87	765.87	118.60	73.50	555.39
4	JA	Reed	Credit Transfer	Weekly	1000L	N	A	535.22	535.22	68.60	45.90	357.87
5	JE	Davies	Credit Transfer	Weekly	500L	Y	A	405.48	405.48	61.80	30.30	313.38
6	GD	Abbiati	Credit Transfer	Weekly	1000L	N	A	480.77	480.77	57.60	39.30	359.33
								2,187.34	2,187.34	306.60	189.00	1,585.97

John Davies' payslip is shown at the top of the next page. Jay checks that his increase has been included and notes that the 'Cost of Net Payments' shows the additional gross pay needed to arrive at the net pay bonus of £50.

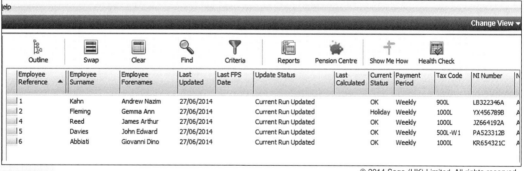

Lock Supplies

Department	-			Payment Method - Credit Transfer			Payment Period - Weekly	
Cost of Net Payments	1.00	23.6800	23.68	PAYE Tax		61.80	Total Gross Pay TD	3821.48
Warehouse basic	35.00	8.4000	294.00	National Insurance		30.30	Gross for Tax TD	3821.48
Warehouse overtime	3.00	12.6000	37.80				Tax paid TD	396.00
Bonus	1.00	50.0000	50.00				Earnings For NI TD	3821.00
							National Insurance TD	238.44
							Earnings for NI	405.00
							Gross for Tax	405.48
							Total Gross Pay	405.48
							Nat. Insurance No	PA523312B

| 12 | 27/06/2014 | | | 500L W1 | 5 | Mr. JE Davies | | 313.38 |

Jay can now Backup and Update the records for Week 12 payroll.

The employee list on the payroll screen looks like this after the payroll has been updated and current year leavers excluded (see tip on page 93 for how to do this).

	Outline	Swap	Clear	Find	Criteria	Reports	Pension Centre	Show Me How	Health Check					
	Employee Reference ▲	Employee Surname	Employee Forenames	Last Updated	Last FPS Date	Update Status		Last Calculated	Current Status	Payment Period	Tax Code	NI Number	N
1	Kahn	Andrew Nazim	27/06/2014		Current Run Updated		OK	Weekly	900L	LB322346A	A
2	Fleming	Gemma Ann	27/06/2014		Current Run Updated		Holiday	Weekly	1000L	YX456789B	A
4	Reed	James Arthur	27/06/2014		Current Run Updated		OK	Weekly	1000L	JZ664192A	A
5	Davies	John Edward	27/06/2014		Current Run Updated		OK	Weekly	500L-W1	PA523312B	A
6	Abbiati	Giovanni Dino	27/06/2014		Current Run Updated		OK	Weekly	1000L	KR654321C	A

RUNNING PERIOD END REPORTS INCLUDING P32

As you have already seen, the payroll software can generate a wide range of reports. You will not use all of them, but it is useful to look at some others that you have not yet come across, especially the P32 monthly report that shows the money due from the business to HMRC at the end of each tax month. This includes tax, National Insurance and student loan repayments.

Tax months are not the same as calendar months. A tax month stretches from 6th of one month to the 5th of the next. So for June the tax month stretches from 6 June to 5 July.

The total on the P32 form has to be paid to HMRC by the 19th of the month following the month of the payroll (or 22nd if paid by credit transfer), so for payrolls in the tax month of June any amount due must be paid by 19th or 22nd July. Some small employers with low monthly liability can pay quarterly (every three months) instead of monthly.

Other statutory deductions must be paid monthly to the agencies that collect them. For example, Attachment of Earnings Orders (AEOs) must be paid to the courts. A report showing how much is owed can be printed.

Case Study

Jay has now completed four payrolls – from tax Week 9 to tax Week 12. These weeks are all in tax month 3 (June).

Jay clicks on Payroll and then on Reports in the horizontal toolbar. Then she clicks on the category called Period End. She chooses Form P32 – Employers Payment Record.

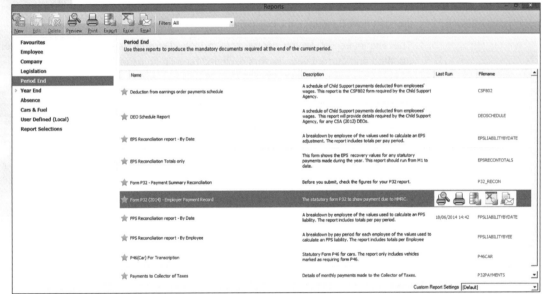

In the criteria box, she inserts tax months 3 and 3. This will show only the values for June (month 3).

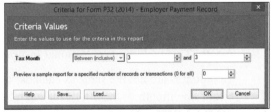

She selects the check box on the next screen to update the HMRC payments log in Company Settings. The top part of the P32 is shown below.

To record the P32 totals in Company Settings, select the check box below.

Update the Payments ☑

Note: Do not select this check box if you use the Collector of Taxes Wizard to make payments to HMRC, as this automatically updates the information.

OK

Date :

Time :

Lock Supplies

Form P32 (2014) - Employer Payment Record

| Tax Month From: | 3 | Tax Month To: | 3 |
| Date From: | 06/06/2014 | Date To: | 05/07/2014 |

1 - PAYE Income Tax:	1,284.40	
2 - Student Loan Deductions:	26.00	
3 - Net Income Tax:	1,310.40	(1 + 2)
4 - Gross National Insurance:	1,778.40	
5 - Employment Allowance:	0.00	
6 - Total SMP Recovered:	0.00	
7 - NIC Compensation on SMP (if due):	0.00	
8 - Total SPP Recovered:	0.00	
9 - NIC Compensation on SPP (if due):	0.00	
10 - Total ASPP Recovered:	0.00	
11 - NIC Compensation on ASPP (if due):	0.00	
12 - Total SAP Recovered:	0.00	
13 - NIC Compensation on SAP (if due):	0.00	
14 - Total NIC Deductions:	0.00	
15 - Net National Insurance:	1,778.40	(4 minus 5 minus 14)
16 - Employer NI to Pay:	997.00	
17 - Total Amount Due:	3,088.80	(3 + 15)

Note: the tax month of June 2014 (6 June to 5 July) has five Fridays in it. It is unusual for there to be five weekly paydays in a month, but it does happen. The P32 should be run again after the fifth payroll on Friday 4 July to give a complete picture.

Jay could also see how much has been deducted from James Reed's pay in the way of AEOs.

She clicks on Employee/Reports/Employee/Attachment History. In the Criteria box she just clicks OK.

Date :					Page :	1 of 1
Time :		**Lock Supplies**				
		Attachment History				

	Employee Ref From :	1	Process Date From :	06/04/2014
	Employee Ref To :	9,999,999	Process Date To :	05/04/2015

EMPLOYEE :   4 - JA   Reed

1 - Child Support

Process Date	Attachable Earnings This Period	Total Value Of Attachment	Paid This Period	Paid To Date	Admin Cost This Period
20/06/2014	370.72	0.00	50.00	50.00	0.00
27/06/2014	420.72		50.00	100.00	0.00

Tip – Checking employee payment history

A cumulative record of payment details builds up in the record of each employee. Choose any of the original employees of the Company (Refs 1-5), open their Employee Record and click on the History tab. The screen displays all the gross and net pay details to date for the current tax year. For more details click on the View P11 button. This screen gives full details of PAYE and NI deductions to date.

More history is available via the Employment tab. Click the YTD Values button and have a browse.

Chapter Summary

■ A business might want to ensure that net pay rather than gross pay is increased by a given amount, for example when a bonus payment is given. The program will gross up the net pay to include any tax or NI, and arrive at a gross pay figure.

■ Pay rates for individual employees can be updated or changed in their employee record. This may be the result of promotion or cost of living increase.

■ All statutory deductions must be remitted to HMRC at regular intervals, usually monthly. The amount due is shown on a P32 Employer Payment Record report, one of a range of period-end reports.

■ Any amounts due to outside agencies should be calculated and remitted.

Key Terms

bonus	pay in addition to normal pay. Sometimes used to reward staff for good results or for a particular event, eg Christmas
P32	a form giving details of money due to HMRC at the end of a tax month. This includes tax, National Insurance and student loan repayments deducted from employees' pay

Activities

1   Set up a £50 net pay bonus for all eligible staff (everyone except Giovanni) (page 91). Take a screenshot showing the set up screen (page 91).

2   Increase John Davies' pay rates to £8.40 Basic and £12.60 Overtime (page 92).

3   Enter payments for Week 12 (pages 93-94).

4   Print (or save) an Update Records Check Report (page 94) and check it against the one on page 94.

5   Print (or save) payslips (page 95). Check John Davies' payslip against the one on page 95.

6   Run the payroll for Week 12 ensuring that all eligible staff receive the £50 net pay bonus (page 96).

7   Run two reports: P32 Employer Payment Record for June and Attachment History for James Reed (pages 97-98).

Practice assessment
Sound Design

This practice exercise is set in the tax year 2014-15 so the suggested answers show figures for that year. If you need to change the settings for the software being used, please amend the parameters for tax and NI as shown below.

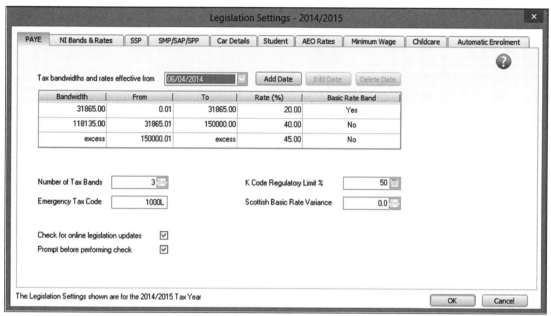

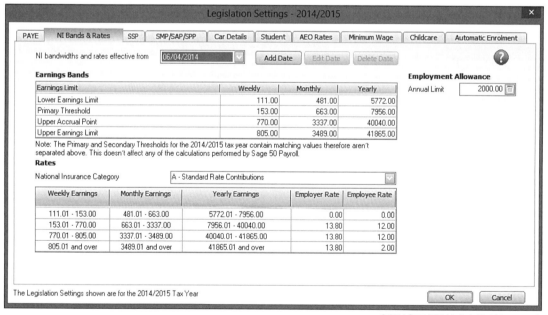

You have taken over the payroll for Sound Design, a business that provides studio recording facilities for musicians and film-makers.

There are four full-time employees and one part-time employee.

Full-time employees receive agreed basic pay for working a 37.5 hour week from Mon-Fri. Overtime is paid for any hours worked over and above 37.5 hours on weekdays and for any work on Saturdays.

Employees are paid fortnightly on a Friday for the 14-day period ending on the previous Wednesday. The next payday is Friday of Week 22. This covers the two week period up to Wednesday of Week 22, shown as Weeks 21 and 22 on the timesheets.

Task 1

(a)   Enter the following business details:

Sound Design
35 Himley Road
Tooting
London
SW17 9BB

Tax Dist / Ref: 075 / T1650

Accounts Office Ref: 075 PC 99887766

(b)   Set up the following pay rates:

Engineer Overtime	£13.00 per hour
Trainee Overtime	£10.30 per hour
Administration assistant	£9.00 per hour
Expenses	Variable

(c)   Pay deductions:

Private Medical Insurance	Variable

> **Backup with your own filename whenever you see this prompt: BACKUP**

Task 2

Set up the following existing employees from the information below. You can assume that if a field is not shown here it can be ignored or is not relevant. All employees are paid by credit transfer and all are category A for NI.

EMPLOYEE 1

Title	Ms	Payment Frequency	Fortnightly
Surname	Miller	Tax Code	1000L
Forenames	Alexis	NI Number	JZ664192A
Address	45 Khartoum Square Tooting London	NI Category	A
		Student loan	Yes
Postcode	SW17 0FY	Job title	Owner/Manager
Marital Status	Single	Pay rate (salary)	£500 per week
Sex	Female	Payment Name	Expenses
Date of Birth	24/03/1984	Deduction Name	Private Medical Ins
Employee Start Date	01/08/11	Rate	£10 per week
Payment Method	Credit transfer		

EMPLOYEE 2

Title	Mr	Payment Method	Credit transfer
Surname	Smith	Payment Frequency	Fortnightly
Forenames	Daniel Paul	Tax Code	950L
Address	Flat 14 Common Place Clapham London	NI Number	PJ105298B
		NI Category	A
		Job title	Sound engineer
Postcode	SW4 7DD	Pay rate (salary)	£320 per week
Marital Status	Single	Payment Name	Engineer overtime
Sex	Male	Rate	£13.00 per hour
Date of Birth	05/07/1982		
Employee Start Date	01/08/11		

EMPLOYEE 3

Title	Mrs	Payment Method	Credit transfer
Surname	Ryan	Payment Frequency	Fortnightly
Forenames	Mary Jane	Tax Code	628L
Address	8 Church Close Wimbledon London	NI Number	YZ224855B
		NI Category	A
Postcode	SW19 4LR	Job title	Administration Manager
Marital Status	Married	Pay rate	£450 per week
Sex	Female		
Date of Birth	25/01/60		
Employee Start Date	01/01/12		

EMPLOYEE 4

Title	Mr	Payment Method	Credit transfer
Surname	Singh	Payment Frequency	Fortnightly
Forenames	Upjeet	Tax Code	1000L
Address	103 Broadway Stockwell	NI Number	NB983327A
		NI Category	A
Postcode	SW9 1XP	Job title	Trainee engineer
Marital Status	Single	Pay rate (salary)	£240 per week
Sex	Male	Payment Name	Trainee overtime
Date of Birth	17/07/94	Rate	£10.30 per hour
Employee Start Date	08/02/2013		

EMPLOYEE 5

Title	Ms	Payment Method	Credit transfer
Surname	Otieno	Payment Frequency	Fortnightly
Forenames	Jama	Tax Code	1000L
Address	14 Thomas Road Earlsfield London	NI Number	BB526419D
		NI Category	A
Postcode	SW18 4ST	Job title	Administration assistant (part-time)
Marital Status	Divorced	Pay rate	£9.00 per hour for all hours worked
Sex	Female		
Date of Birth	05/07/70		
Employee Start Date	01/06/2012		

BACKUP

Task 3

(a) As at Week 20 these are the employees' year to date figures. Enter these into the program.

Employee	Gross pay (all) £	Tax paid £	Up to LEL £	LEL to PT £	PT to UAP £	UAP to UEL £	Ee NIC £	Er NIC £
A Miller	10000.00	1230.80	2220.00	840.00	6940.00	0.00	832.80	957.72
D Smith	7360.00	741.20	2220.00	840.00	4300.00	0.00	516.00	593.40
M Ryan	9000.00	1316.80	2220.00	840.00	5940.00	0.00	712.80	819.72
U Singh	5390.00	308.60	2220.00	840.00	2330.00	0.00	279.60	321.54
J Otieno	2880.00	0.00	2220.00	840.00	0.00	0.00	0.00	0.00

(b) Print reports showing the following:
  • employees' personal details including start date
  • employees' tax and NI figures to date

(c) **BACKUP**
Backup and print a screenshot of the backup screen showing the filename.

Task 4

(a)   Set up an employee record for a new employee who started on Monday of Week 22.

EMPLOYEE 6				
Title	Miss		Payment Method	Credit transfer
Surname	Perez		Payment Frequency	Fortnightly
Forenames	Calida		From P45	See below
Address	42 Mitcham Road		Starting declaration	None
	Tooting		NI Number	NL256257B
	London			
Postcode	SW17 2PS		NI Category	A
Marital Status	Single		Job title	Trainee technician
Sex	Female		Pay rate (salary)	£240 per week
			Payment Name	Trainee overtime
Date of Birth	19/09/95		Rate	£10.30 per hour
Employee Start Date	01/09/14			

P45 INFORMATION	
Previous tax distr ref	070/24570
Date left prev employment	01/08/14
Total pay to date	£3920.00
Total tax to date	£130.00
Tax code	1000L

(b)   Daniel Smith has advised a change of home address. His new address is:

7 The Mews
Rodenhurst Road
Clapham
London
SW4 5RN

(c)   Print the following report for Calida Perez and Daniel Smith only.

•   employees' personal details including start date

BACKUP

Tasks 5 to 8 give information relating to the payroll for Week 22. You are to:

- *ensure that the process date is correct*
- *ensure that basic pay and overtime are correctly calculated and entered*
- *ensure that any additional payments or deductions are entered and processed*
- *prepare the payroll (but do not update records yet)*

Task 5

Alexis has started contributing to a stakeholder pension scheme at the rate of 5% of her pay from Week 22. There is no employer contribution. The pension provider is Kinder Assurance, York House, York Street, Huddersfield, West Yorkshire HD1 1RR.

A Miller	Thurs	Fri	Sat	Mon	Tues	Wed	Total hours	
Week 21	7.5	7.5	0	7.5	7.5	7.5	Basic:	Overtime:
Week 22	4	7.5	0	8.5	9	8.5	Basic:	Overtime:
				Totals for fortnight			Basic:	Overtime:
Notes	Alexis is to be paid £79.50 expenses.							
	Pension contribution to be deducted.							
	Private medical insurance to be deducted (2 weeks @ £10 per week).							
	Student loan repayment to be deducted.							

Task 6

Mary is going on holiday for Weeks 23 and 24. She is to receive pay in advance for these holiday weeks.

M Ryan	Thurs	Fri	Sat	Mon	Tues	Wed	Total hours	
Week 21	7.5	7.5	0	7.5	7.5	7.5	Basic:	Overtime:
Week 22	7.5	7.5	0	7.5	7.5	7.5	Basic:	Overtime:
				Totals for fortnight			Basic:	Overtime:
Notes	Private medical insurance to be deducted (2 weeks @ £25 per week).							
	Mary is to receive 2 weeks advanced pay in addition to her pay for Weeks 21 and 22.							
	Private medical insurance to be deducted for these two holiday weeks.							

Task 7

The remaining employees have worked as follows:

D Smith	Thurs	Fri	Sat	Mon	Tues	Wed	Total hours	
Week 21	7.5	7.5	3	7.5	8	8	Basic:	Overtime:
Week 22	7	7.5	0	8	7.5	7.5	Basic:	Overtime:
					Totals for fortnight		Basic:	Overtime:
Notes								

U Singh	Thurs	Fri	Sat	Mon	Tues	Wed	Total hours	
Week 21	7.5	7.5	0	7.5	7.5	7.5	Basic:	Overtime:
Week 22	7.5	7.5	0	7.5	8	8	Basic:	Overtime:
					Totals for fortnight		Basic:	Overtime:
Notes								

J Otieno	Thurs	Fri	Sat	Mon	Tues	Wed	Total hours	
Week 21	4	0	0	4	4	4	Basic:	Overtime:
Week 22	4	0	0	4	4	4	Basic:	Overtime:
					Totals for fortnight		Basic:	Overtime:
Notes								

C Perez	Thurs	Fri	Sat	Mon	Tues	Wed	Total hours	
Week 21	0	0	0	0	0	0	Basic:	Overtime:
Week 22	7	7.5	0	8	7.5	7.5	Basic:	Overtime:
					Totals for fortnight		Basic:	Overtime:
Notes	Calida joined the business at the beginning of Week 22. There is no pay for Week 21. She is likely to receive an automatic refund of tax.							

Task 8

(a)   Print reports showing the following:

- update records check report
- a payment summary which includes all payments to be made (parts 1 & 2)
- a payslip for each employee

(b)   **BACKUP** as part of the updating process.

(c)   Update the records for Week 22 payroll.

- print a screenshot showing your employees' current status after running the payroll

Task 9

(a)   You are to enter the business bank details in the records. They are:

Royal Bank of London
240 Upper Tooting Road
London
SW17 0ED

Telephone: 0845 567 4444

Account name: Sound Design
Account number: 65432198
Sort code: 01-22-33

(b)   Print a report showing the business details including bank details.

BACKUP

Tasks 10 to 15 give information relating to the payroll for Week 24. You are to

- *ensure that the process date is correct*
- *ensure that basic pay and overtime are correctly calculated and entered*
- *ensure that any additional payments or deductions are entered and processed*
- *prepare the payroll (do not update records yet)*

Task 10

A change of tax code notice has been received advising a change of tax code for Alexis Miller with immediate effect from 1000L to 820L Week 1/Month1.

A Miller	Thurs	Fri	Sat	Mon	Tues	Wed	Total hours	
Week 23	7.5	7.5	0	7	8	7.5	Basic:	Overtime:
Week 24	8	7.5	0	7.5	7.5	7	Basic:	Overtime:
					Totals for fortnight		Basic:	Overtime:

Notes	Enter change of tax code.
	Alexis is to be paid £35.90 expenses.
	Pension contribution to be deducted.
	Private medical insurance to be deducted (2 weeks @ £10 per week).
	Student loan repayment to be deducted.

Task 11

Mary Ryan is on holiday. She received advanced pay for Weeks 23 and 24 so there is no pay to process.

Task 12

The business has been doing well over the summer thanks to Daniel's hard work and the extra hours he has put in. Alexis has decided that Daniel should receive a net pay bonus of £100 in his pay for Week 24.

Daniel wants to start giving £10 per week to an approved charity through the GAYE (Payroll Giving) scheme.

D Smith	Thurs	Fri	Sat	Mon	Tues	Wed	Total hours	
Week 23	8	7.5	3	7.5	8	8	Basic:	Overtime:
Week 24	8	7.5	3	7	7.5	7.5	Basic:	Overtime:
				Totals for fortnight			Basic:	Overtime:
Notes	Enter £100 net pay bonus. Enter charity deductions (2 weeks @ £10 per week).							

Task 13

A Council Tax arrears notice has been received relating to Calida Perez. The total amount is £776.20 and the reference is SL04811. It is a Priority 1 order and is effective from 15 September. The tables for Council Tax deductions are to be used (tick the check box for using tables on the AEO tab).

C Perez	Thurs	Fri	Sat	Mon	Tues	Wed	Total hours	
Week 23	7.5	7.5	3	7.5	7.5	7.5	Basic:	Overtime:
Week 24	7	8	3	7.5	7.5	7.5	Basic:	Overtime:
				Totals for fortnight			Basic:	Overtime:
Notes	Council tax AEO to be entered.							

Task 14

The remaining employees have worked as follows:

Upjeet Singh has given notice that he is to leave on Wednesday of Week 24.

U Singh	Thurs	Fri	Sat	Mon	Tues	Wed	Total hours	
Week 23	8.5	7.5	0	7.5	5.5	8.5	Basic:	Overtime:
Week 24	7.5	7.5	0	7.5	7.5	7.5	Basic:	Overtime:
					Totals for fortnight		Basic:	Overtime:
Notes	Upjeet is leaving the business.							

J Otieno	Thurs	Fri	Sat	Mon	Tues	Wed	Total hours	
Week 23	4	0	0	4	4	4	Basic:	Overtime:
Week 24	4	0	0	4	4	4	Basic:	Overtime:
					Totals for fortnight		Basic:	Overtime:
Notes								

Task 15

    (a)   Print reports showing the following:

        •   update records check report

        •   a payment summary which includes all payments to be made (parts 1 & 2)

        •   a payslip for each employee

    (b)   **BACKUP** as part of the updating process.

    (c)   Update the records for Week 24 payroll.

    (d)   Print a P45 for Upjeet Singh.

Task 16

Print reports showing the following:

•   a screenshot showing current status of employees

•   a P32 for Month 6 (to date)

•   attachment details

•   pension provider's name and address

•   a screenshot showing the screen for restoring a backup if you had to use it

Suggested answers

Task 3(b)

Date : Time :		Sound Design **Employee Details - Personal**						Page :	1 of 2				

Tax Week 22   Tax Month 5

Employee Reference	Employee Name, Address, Email & Mobile	Job Title	Employment Status Type	Date of Birth	Marital Status	Sex	Pay Frequency	NI Number	NI Cat	Con Out	Tax Code	W1/ M1	Starter Form	Start Date	Pay Method
1	Alexis Miller 45 Khartoum Square Tooting London SW17 0FY	Owner/Manager		24/03/1984	Single	Female	Fortnightly	JZ664192A	A	N	1000L	N	None	01/08/2011	Credit Transfer
2	Daniel Paul Smith Flat 14 Common Place Clapham London SW4 7DD	Sound engineer		05/07/1982	Single	Male	Fortnightly	PJ105298B	A	N	950L	N	None	01/08/2011	Credit Transfer
3	Mary Jane Ryan 8 Church Close Wimbledon London SW19 4LR	Administration Manager		25/01/1960	Married	Female	Fortnightly	YZ224855B	A	N	628L	N	None	01/01/2012	Credit Transfer

Date : Time :		Sound Design **Employee Details - Personal**						Page :	2 of 2				

Tax Week 22   Tax Month 5

Employee Reference	Employee Name, Address, Email & Mobile	Job Title	Employment Status Type	Date of Birth	Marital Status	Sex	Pay Frequency	NI Number	NI Cat	Con Out	Tax Code	W1/ M1	Starter Form	Start Date	Pay Method
4	Upjeet Singh 103 Broadway Stockwell London SW9 1XP	Trainee engineer		17/07/1994	Single	Male	Fortnightly	NB983327A	A	N	1000L	N	None	08/02/2013	Credit Transfer
5	Jama Otieno 14 Thomas Road Earlsfield London SW18 4ST	Administration assistant		05/07/1970	Divorced	Female	Fortnightly	BB526419D	A	N	1000L	N	None	01/06/2012	Credit Transfer

Date : Time :		Sound Design **Employee Details - Cumulative**							Page :	1 of 1			

Tax Week 20   Tax Month 5

E'ee Ref	Employee Name	SSP	SMP	SPP	SAP	Total Gross	NI'able Earns TD	Taxable Pay	Tax Due To Date	Student Loan	Holiday Fund	Employee NI	Employer NI	Loans	Employee Pension	Employer Pension
1	Ms. A Miller	0.00	0.00	0.00	0.00	10000.00	10000.00	10000.00	1230.80	0.00	0.00	832.80	957.72	0.00	0.00	0.00
2	Mr. DP Smith	0.00	0.00	0.00	0.00	7360.00	7360.00	7360.00	741.20	0.00	0.00	516.00	593.40	0.00	0.00	0.00
3	Mrs. MJ Ryan	0.00	0.00	0.00	0.00	9000.00	9000.00	9000.00	1316.80	0.00	0.00	712.80	819.72	0.00	0.00	0.00
4	Mr. U Singh	0.00	0.00	0.00	0.00	5390.00	5390.00	5390.00	308.60	0.00	0.00	279.60	321.54	0.00	0.00	0.00
5	Ms. J Otieno	0.00	0.00	0.00	0.00	2880.00	3060.00	2880.00	0.00	0.00	0.00	0.00	0.00	0.00	0.00	0.00
	Totals :	0.00	0.00	0.00	0.00	34630.00	34810.00	34630.00	3597.40	0.00	0.00	2341.20	2692.38	0.00	0.00	0.00

Task 3(c)

Screenshot of backup showing filename. (Not shown here.)

Task 4(c)

Date : Time :			Sound Design Employee Details - Personal Tax Week 22 Tax Month 5											Page : 1 of 1		
Employee Reference	Employee Name, Address, Email & Mobile	Job Title	Employment Status Type	Date of Birth	Marital Status	Sex	Pay Frequency	NI Number	NI Cat	Con Out	Tax Code	W1/ M1	Starter Form	Start Date	Pay Method
2	Daniel Paul Smith 7 The Mews Rodenhurst Road Clapham London SW4 5RN	Sound engineer		05/07/1982	Single	Male	Fortnightly	PJ105298B	A	N	950L	N	None	01/08/2011	Credit Transfer
6	Calida Perez 42 Mitcham Road Tooting London SW17 2PS	Trainee technician		19/09/1995	Single	Female	Fortnightly	NL256257B	A	N	1000L	N	P45	01/09/2014	Credit Transfer

Task 8(a)

Date : Time :			Sound Design Update Records Check Report Tax Month : 5 Week : 22										Page : 1 of 1	
Ref	Name		Payment Method	Payment Frequency	Tax Code	W1/ M1	NI Cat	Total Gross	Taxable Gross	Tax Paid	Employee NIC	Net Pay
1	A	Miller	Credit Transfer	Fortnightly	1000L	N	A	1,079.50	1,000.00	122.20	83.40	783.90
2	DP	Smith	Credit Transfer	Fortnightly	950L	N	A	692.00	692.00	64.40	46.44	581.16
3	MJ	Ryan	Credit Transfer	Fortnightly	628L	N	A	1,800.00	1,800.00	262.60	142.80	1,294.60
4	U	Singh	Credit Transfer	Fortnightly	1000L	N	A	490.30	490.30	20.40	22.20	447.70
5	J	Otieno	Credit Transfer	Fortnightly	1000L	N	A	288.00	288.00	0.00	0.00	288.00
6	C	Perez	Credit Transfer	Fortnightly	1000L	N	A	240.00	240.00	-130.00	0.00	370.00
								4,589.80	4,510.30	339.60	294.84	3,765.36

Task 8(a) continued

| Date: | | | | | | Sound Design | | | | | | | | Page: | 1 of 1 | | | |
| Time: | | | | | | Payment Summary (Part 1) Landscape | | | | | | | | | | | | |

Tax Month : 5   Week : 22   Payment Frequency: Fortnightly

E'ee Ref	Employee Name	Total Gross	Taxable Gross	Pre-Tax Payment	Pre-Tax Ded'n	Student Loan	PAYE	Employee NIC	Employee Pension*	SSP	SMP	SPP	ASPP	SAP	Post-Tax Payment	Post-Tax Ded'n	B/F	C/F	Net Pay
1	A Miller	1079.50	1000.00	1000.00	0.00	30.00	122.20	83.40	40.00	0.00	0.00	0.00	0.00	0.00	79.50	20.00	0.00	0.00	783.90
2	DP Smith	692.00	692.00	692.00	0.00	0.00	64.40	46.44	0.00	0.00	0.00	0.00	0.00	0.00	0.00	0.00	0.00	0.00	581.16
3	MJ Ryan	1800.00	1800.00	1800.00	0.00	0.00	262.60	142.80	0.00	0.00	0.00	0.00	0.00	0.00	100.00	0.00	0.00	0.00	1294.60
4	U Singh	490.30	490.30	490.30	0.00	0.00	20.40	22.20	0.00	0.00	0.00	0.00	0.00	0.00	0.00	0.00	0.00	0.00	447.70
5	J Otieno	288.00	288.00	288.00	0.00	0.00	0.00	0.00	0.00	0.00	0.00	0.00	0.00	0.00	0.00	0.00	0.00	0.00	288.00
6	C Perez	240.00	240.00	240.00	0.00	0.00	-130.00	0.00	0.00	0.00	0.00	0.00	0.00	0.00	0.00	0.00	0.00	0.00	370.00
6	Employees	4589.80	4510.30	4510.30	0.00	30.00	339.60	294.84	40.00	0.00	0.00	0.00	0.00	0.00	79.50	120.00	0.00	0.00	3765.36

*Please note this value does not include any contribution made to a salary sacrifice pension scheme.

| Date: | | | | | | | | Sound Design | | | | | Page: | 1 of 1 | | |
| Time: | | | | | | | | Payment Summary (Part 2) Landscape | | | | | | | | |

Tax Month : 5   Week : 22   Payment Frequency: Fortnightly

E'ee Ref	Employee Name	NI'able Earnings	E'ee + E'er NI Contribution	Employer NI Contribution	Employee NI Contribution	Employer NI Rebate	Employee NI Rebate	Employer Pension*	Tax Code	Week 1 / Month 1	NI Cat	Con Out
1	A Miller	1,000.00	179.30	95.90	83.40	0.00	0.00	0.00	1000L	N	A	N
2	DP Smith	692.00	99.84	53.40	46.44	0.00	0.00	0.00	950L	N	A	N
3	MJ Ryan	1,800.00	307.00	164.20	142.80	0.00	0.00	0.00	628L	N	A	N
4	U Singh	490.00	47.72	25.52	22.20	0.00	0.00	0.00	1000L	N	A	N
5	J Otieno	288.00	0.00	0.00	0.00	0.00	0.00	0.00	1000L	N	A	N
6	C Perez	240.00	0.00	0.00	0.00	0.00	0.00	0.00	1000L	N	A	N
6	Employees	£4,510.00	£633.86	£339.02	£294.84	£0.00	£0.00	£0.00				

*For salary sacrifice pension schemes this is the employer contribution including the amount sacrificed by the employee.

Sound Design

Department	-				Payment Method - Credit Transfer		Payment Period - Fortnightly	
Salary	1.00	1000.0000	1000.00		PAYE Tax	122.20	Total Gross Pay TD	11079.50
Expenses	1.00	79.5000	79.50		National Insurance	83.40	Gross for Tax TD	11000.00
					Ee Pension	40.00	Tax paid TD	1353.00
							Earnings For NI TD	11000.00
					Student Loan	30.00	National Insurance TD	916.20
							Ee Pension TD	40.00
					Private medical insur	20.00		
							Earnings for NI	1000.00
							Gross for Tax	1000.00
							Total Gross Pay	1079.50
							Nat. Insurance No	JZ664192A

| 22 | 05/09/2014 | | 1000L | 1 | Ms. A Miller | 783.90 |

Sound Design

Department	-				Payment Method - Credit Transfer		Payment Period - Fortnightly	
Salary	1.00	640.0000	640.00		PAYE Tax	64.40	Total Gross Pay TD	8052.00
Engineer overtime	4.00	13.0000	52.00		National Insurance	46.44	Gross for Tax TD	8052.00
							Tax paid TD	805.60
							Earnings For NI TD	8052.00
							National Insurance TD	562.44
							Earnings for NI	692.00
							Gross for Tax	692.00
							Total Gross Pay	692.00
							Nat. Insurance No	PJ105298B

22	05/09/2014			950L	2	Mr. DP Smith	581.16

Sound Design

Department	-				Payment Method - Credit Transfer		Payment Period - Fortnightly	
Salary	1.00	900.0000	900.00		PAYE Tax	262.60	Total Gross Pay TD	10800.00
					National Insurance	142.80	Gross for Tax TD	10800.00
							Tax paid TD	1579.40
							Earnings For NI TD	10800.00
							National Insurance TD	855.60
					Private medical insur	100.00		
Advance Pay			900.00				Earnings for NI	1800.00
							Gross for Tax	1800.00
							Total Gross Pay	1800.00
							Nat. Insurance No	YZ224855B

22	05/09/2014			628L	3	Mrs. MJ Ryan	1294.60

Sound Design

Department	-				Payment Method - Credit Transfer		Payment Period - Fortnightly	
Salary	1.00	480.0000	480.00		PAYE Tax	20.40	Total Gross Pay TD	5880.30
Trainee overtime	1.00	10.3000	10.30		National Insurance	22.20	Gross for Tax TD	5880.30
							Tax paid TD	329.00
							Earnings For NI TD	5880.00
							National Insurance TD	301.80
							Earnings for NI	490.00
							Gross for Tax	490.30
							Total Gross Pay	490.30
							Nat. Insurance No	NB983327A

22	05/09/2014			1000L	4	Mr. U Singh	447.70

Task 8(a) continued

Sound Design

Department	-			Payment Method - Credit Transfer		Payment Period - Fortnightly	
Administration assistant	32.00	9.0000	288.00	PAYE Tax	0.00	Total Gross Pay TD	3168.00
				National Insurance	0.00	Gross for Tax TD	3168.00
						Tax paid TD	0.00
						Earnings For NI TD	3348.00
						National Insurance TD	0.00
						Earnings for NI	288.00
						Gross for Tax	288.00
						Total Gross Pay	288.00
						Nat. Insurance No	BB526419D

22	05/09/2014			1000L	5	Ms. J Otieno	288.00

Sound Design

Department	-			Payment Method - Credit Transfer		Payment Period - Fortnightly	
Salary	1.00	240.0000	240.00	PAYE Tax	-130.00	Total Gross Pay TD	4160.00
				National Insurance	0.00	Gross for Tax TD	4160.00
						Tax paid TD	0.00
						Earnings For NI TD	240.00
						National Insurance TD	0.00
						Earnings for NI	240.00
						Gross for Tax	240.00
						Total Gross Pay	240.00
						Nat. Insurance No	NL256257B

22	05/09/2014			1000L	6	Miss. C Perez	370.00

Task 8(c)

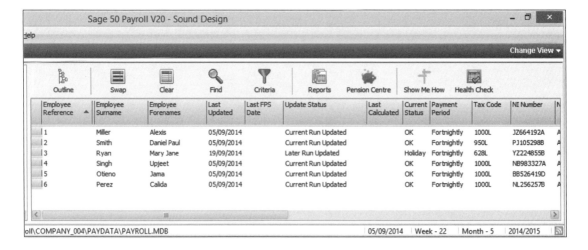

Employee Reference	Employee Surname	Employee Forenames	Last Updated	Last FPS Date	Update Status	Last Calculated	Current Status	Payment Period	Tax Code	NI Number	N
1	Miller	Alexis	05/09/2014		Current Run Updated		OK	Fortnightly	1000L	JZ664192A	A
2	Smith	Daniel Paul	05/09/2014		Current Run Updated		OK	Fortnightly	950L	PJ105298B	A
3	Ryan	Mary Jane	19/09/2014		Later Run Updated		Holiday	Fortnightly	628L	YZ224855B	A
4	Singh	Upjeet	05/09/2014		Current Run Updated		OK	Fortnightly	1000L	NB983327A	A
5	Otieno	Jama	05/09/2014		Current Run Updated		OK	Fortnightly	1000L	BB526419D	A
6	Perez	Calida	05/09/2014		Current Run Updated		OK	Fortnightly	1000L	NL256257B	A

oll\COMPANY_004\PAYDATA\PAYROLL.MDB   05/09/2014   Week - 22   Month - 5   2014/2015

Task 9(b)

Date :		Sound Design	Page :	1 of 1
Time :		Company Details		

Name :		**Sound Design**	
Address :		35 Himley Road	
		Tooting	
		London	
Post Code :		SW17 9BB	
Telephone :			
Fax :			
E-Mail Address :			
Tax District :		075	
Tax Reference :		T1650	
Bank Name :		Royal Bank of London	
Address :		240 Upper Tooting Road	
		London	
Post Code :		SW17 0ED	
Telephone :		0845 567 4444	
Fax :			
E-Mail Address :			
Bank Sort Code :		01-22-33	
Bank Account Number :		65432198	
Bank Account Name :		Sound Design	
Building Society Number :			
BACS Reference :			
Account Type :		Bank Account	
IBAN :			
BIC :			
ECON :		E	

Task 15(a)

Date :		Sound Design							Page :	1 of 1	
Time :		Update Records Check Report									
		Tax Month : 6 Week : 24									

Ref	Name		Payment Method	Payment Frequency	Tax Code	W1/ M1	NI Cat	Total Gross	Taxable Gross	Tax Paid	Employee NIC	Net Pay
1	A	Miller	Credit Transfer	Fortnightly	820L	Y	A	1,035.90	1,000.00	136.80	83.40	725.70
2	DP	Smith	Credit Transfer	Fortnightly	950L	N	A	884.66	864.66	99.80	69.48	695.38
4	U	Singh	Credit Transfer	Fortnightly	1000L	N	A	480.00	480.00	19.00	21.00	440.00
5	J	Otieno	Credit Transfer	Fortnightly	1000L	N	A	288.00	288.00	0.00	0.00	288.00
6	C	Perez	Credit Transfer	Fortnightly	1000L	N	A	541.80	541.80	16.40	28.20	437.54
								3,230.36	3,174.46	272.00	202.08	2,586.62

Date:		Sound Design																Page:	1 of 1		
Time:		Payment Summary (Part 1) Landscape																			
		Tax Month : 6 Week : 24 Payment Frequency: Fortnightly																			

E'ee Ref	Employee Name	Total Gross	Taxable Gross	Pre-Tax Payment	Pre-Tax Ded'n	Student Loan	PAYE	Employee NIC	Employee Pension*	SSP	SMP	SPP	ASPP	SAP	Post-Tax Payment	Post-Tax Ded'n	B/F	C/F	Net Pay
1	A Miller	1035.90	1000.00	1000.00	0.00	30.00	136.80	83.40	40.00	0.00	0.00	0.00	0.00	0.00	35.90	20.00	0.00	0.00	725.70
2	DP Smith	884.66	864.66	884.66	20.00	0.00	99.80	69.48	0.00	0.00	0.00	0.00	0.00	0.00	0.00	0.00	0.00	0.00	695.38
4	U Singh	480.00	480.00	480.00	0.00	0.00	19.00	21.00	0.00	0.00	0.00	0.00	0.00	0.00	0.00	0.00	0.00	0.00	440.00
5	J Otieno	288.00	288.00	288.00	0.00	0.00	0.00	0.00	0.00	0.00	0.00	0.00	0.00	0.00	0.00	0.00	0.00	0.00	288.00
6	C Perez	541.80	541.80	541.80	0.00	0.00	16.40	28.20	0.00	0.00	0.00	0.00	0.00	0.00	0.00	59.66	0.00	0.00	437.54
5	Employees	3230.36	3174.46	3194.46	20.00	30.00	272.00	202.08	40.00	0.00	0.00	0.00	0.00	0.00	35.90	79.66	0.00	0.00	2586.62

*Please note this value does not include any contribution made to a salary sacrifice pension scheme.

Date:		Sound Design											Page:	1 of 1	
Time:		Payment Summary (Part 2) Landscape													
		Tax Month : 6 Week : 24 Payment Frequency: Fortnightly													

E'ee Ref	Employee Name	NI'able Earnings	E'ee + E'er NI Contribution	Employer NI Contribution	Employee NI Contribution	Employer NI Rebate	Employee NI Rebate	Employer Pension*	Tax Code	Week 1 / Month 1	NI Cat	Con Out
1	A Miller	1,000.00	179.30	95.90	83.40	0.00	0.00	0.00	820L	Y	A	N
2	DP Smith	884.00	149.38	79.90	69.48	0.00	0.00	0.00	950L	N	A	N
4	U Singh	480.00	45.14	24.14	21.00	0.00	0.00	0.00	1000L	N	A	N
5	J Otieno	288.00	0.00	0.00	0.00	0.00	0.00	0.00	1000L	N	A	N
6	C Perez	540.00	60.62	32.42	28.20	0.00	0.00	0.00	1000L	N	A	N
5	Employees	£3,192.00	£434.44	£232.36	£202.08	£0.00	£0.00	£0.00				

*For salary sacrifice pension schemes this is the employer contribution including the amount sacrificed by the employee.

Sound Design

Department	-				Payment Method - Credit Transfer		Payment Period - Fortnightly	
Salary	1.00	1000.0000	1000.00		PAYE Tax	136.80	Total Gross Pay TD	12115.40
Expenses	1.00	35.9000	35.90		National Insurance	83.40	Gross for Tax TD	12000.00
					Ee Pension	40.00	Tax paid TD	1489.80
							Earnings For NI TD	12000.00
					Student Loan	30.00	National Insurance TD	999.60
							Ee Pension TD	80.00
					Private medical insur	20.00		
							Earnings for NI	1000.00
							Gross for Tax	1000.00
							Total Gross Pay	1035.90
							Nat. Insurance No	JZ664192A

24	19/09/2014			820L W1	1	Ms. A Miller	725.70

Sound Design

Department	-				Payment Method - Credit Transfer		Payment Period - Fortnightly	
Salary	1.00	640.0000	640.00		PAYE Tax	99.80	Total Gross Pay TD	8936.66
Cost of Net Payments	1.00	47.1600	47.16		National Insurance	69.48	Gross for Tax TD	8916.66
Engineer overtime	7.50	13.0000	97.50				Tax paid TD	905.40
Net pay bonus	1.00	100.0000	100.00				Earnings For NI TD	8936.00
							National Insurance TD	631.92
					Charity donation	20.00		
							Earnings for NI	884.00
							Gross for Tax	864.66
							Total Gross Pay	884.66
							Nat. Insurance No	PJ105298B

24	19/09/2014			950L	2	Mr. DP Smith	695.38

Sound Design

Department	-				Payment Method - Credit Transfer		Payment Period - Fortnightly	
Salary	1.00	480.0000	480.00		PAYE Tax	19.00	Total Gross Pay TD	6360.30
					National Insurance	21.00	Gross for Tax TD	6360.30
							Tax paid TD	348.00
							Earnings For NI TD	6360.00
							National Insurance TD	322.80
							Earnings for NI	480.00
							Gross for Tax	480.00
							Total Gross Pay	480.00
							Nat. Insurance No	NB983327A

24	19/09/2014			1000L	4	Mr. U Singh	440.00

Task 15(a) continued

Sound Design							
Department -				**Payment Method** - Credit Transfer		**Payment Period** - Fortnightly	
Administration assistant	32.00	9.0000	288.00	PAYE Tax	0.00	Total Gross Pay TD	3456.00
				National Insurance	0.00	Gross for Tax TD	3456.00
						Tax paid TD	0.00
						Earnings For NI TD	3636.00
						National Insurance TD	0.00
						Earnings for NI	288.00
						Gross for Tax	288.00
						Total Gross Pay	288.00
						Nat. Insurance No	BB526419D
24	19/09/2014			1000L	5	Ms. J Otieno	288.00

Sound Design							
Department -				**Payment Method** - Credit Transfer		**Payment Period** - Fortnightly	
Salary	1.00	480.0000	480.00	PAYE Tax	16.40	Total Gross Pay TD	4701.80
Trainee overtime	6.00	10.3000	61.80	National Insurance	28.20	Gross for Tax TD	4701.80
						Tax paid TD	16.40
						Earnings For NI TD	780.00
						National Insurance TD	28.20
						Earnings for NI	540.00
						Gross for Tax	541.80
				Council Tax	59.66	Total Gross Pay	541.80
						Nat. Insurance No	NL256257B
24	19/09/2014			1000L	6	Miss. C Perez	437.54

Task 15(d)

HM Revenue & Customs

P45 Part 1A
Details of employee leaving work
Copy for employee

1 Employer PAYE reference

Office number   Reference number

075 / T1650

2 Employee's National Insurance number

NB 98 33 27 A

3 Title - enter MR, MRS, MISS, MS or other title

Mr.

Surname or family name

Singh

First or given name(s)

Upjeet

4 Leaving date DD MM YYYY

17   09   2014

5 Student Loan deductions

☐ Student Loan deductions to continue

6 Tax Code at leaving date

1000L

If week 1 or month 1 applies, enter 'X' in the box below.

Week 1/Month 1 ☐

7 Last entries on P11 Deductions Working Sheet.
Complete only if Tax Code is cumulative. If there is an 'X' at box 6 there will be no entries here.

Week number 24   Month number ☐

Total pay to date

£ 6360.30 p

Total tax to date

£ 348.00 p

8 This employment pay and tax. If no entry here, the amounts are those shown at box 7.

Total pay in this employment

£ ☐ p

Total tax in this employment

£ ☐ p

9 Works number/Payroll number and Department or branch (if any)

4

10 Gender. Enter 'X' in the appropriate box

Male X   Female ☐

11 Date of birth DD MM YYYY

17   07   1994

12 Employee's private address

103 Broadway
Stockwell
London

Postcode

SW9 1XP

13 I certify that the details entered in items 1 to 11 on this form are correct.

Employer name and address

Sound Design
35 Himley Road
Tooting
London

Postcode

SW17 9BB

Date DD MM YYYY

☐ ☐ ☐

To the employee
The P45 is in three parts. Please keep this part (Part1A) safe. Copies are not available. You might need the information in Part 1A to fill in a Tax Return if you are sent one.

Please read the notes in Part 2 that accompany Part 1A. The notes give some important information about what you should do next and what you should do with Parts 2 and 3 of this form.

P45(Online) Part 1 A

Tax Credits
Tax credits are flexible. They adapt to changes in your life, such as leaving a job. If you need to let us know about a change in your income, phone **0845 300 3900**.

To the new employer
If your new employee gives you this Part 1A, please return it to them. Deal with Parts 2 and 3 as normal.

HMRC 10/08

Task 15(d) continued

HM Revenue & Customs

P45 Part 2
Details of employee leaving work
Copy for new employer

---

1 Employer PAYE reference

Office number   *Reference number*

075 / T1650

2 Employee's National Insurance number

NB 98 33 27 A

3 Title - enter MR, MRS, MISS, MS or other title

Mr.

Surname or family name

Singh

First or given name(s)

Upjeet

4 Leaving date *DD MM YYYY*

1 7   0 9   2 0 1 4

5 Student Loan deductions

☐ Student Loan deductions to continue

6 Tax Code at leaving date

1000L

If week 1 or month 1 applies, enter 'X' in the box below.

Week 1/Month 1   ☐

7 Last entries on P11 *Deductions Working Sheet*.
Complete only if Tax Code is cumulative. If there is an 'X'
at box 6 there will be no entries here.

Week number   24   Month number   ☐

Total pay to date

£   6360.30 p

Total tax to date

£   348.00 p

To the employee

This form is important to you. Take good care of it and
keep it safe. Copies are not available. Please keep
Parts 2 and 3 of the form together and do not alter them
in any way.

Going to a new job

Give Parts 2 and 3 of this form to your new employer,
or you will have tax deducted using the emergency
code and may pay too much tax. If you do not want
your new employer to know the details on this form,
send it to your HM Revenue & Customs (HMRC) office
immediately with a letter saying so and giving the
name and address of your new employer. HMRC can
make special arrangements, but you may pay too
much tax for a while as a result of this.

Going abroad

If you are going abroad or returning to a country
outside the UK ask for form P85 *Leaving the United Kingdom*
from any HMRC office or Enquiry Centre.

Becoming self-employed

You must register with HMRC within three months of
becoming self-employed or you could incur a penalty.
To register as newly self-employed see The Phone Book
under HM Revenue & Customs or go to **www.hmrc.gov.uk**
to get a copy of the booklet SE1 *Are you thinking of working
for yourself?*

Claiming Jobseeker's Allowance or
Employment and Support Allowance (ESA)

Take this form to your Jobcentre Plus Office. They will pay you
any tax refund you may be entitled to when your claim ends,
or at 5 April if this is earlier.

Not working and claiming Jobseeker's Allowance or
Employment and Support Allowance (ESA)

If you have paid tax and wish to claim a refund ask for
form P50 *Claiming tax back when you have stopped working*
from any HMRC office or Enquiry Centre.

Help

If you need further help you can contact any HMRC office
or Enquiry Centre. You can find us in The Phone Book under
HM Revenue & Customs or go to **www.hmrc.gov.uk**

To the new employer

Check this form and complete boxes 8 to 18 in Part 3
and prepare a form P11 *Deductions Working Sheet*.
Follow the instructions in the Employer Helpbook
E13 Day-to-day payroll, for how to prepare a P11 *Deductions
Working Sheet*. Send Part 3 of this form to your HMRC
office immediately. Keep Part 2.

P45 Part 3
New employee details
For completion by new employer

File your employee's P45 online at **www.hmrc.gov.uk**

Use capital letters when completing this form

1 Employer PAYE reference

Office number   *Reference number*

075 / T1650

5 Student Loan deductions

☐ Student Loan deductions to continue

6 Tax Code at leaving date

1000L

If week 1 or month 1 applies, enter 'X' in the box below.

Week 1/Month 1   ☐

2 Employee's National Insurance number

NB 98 33 27 A

3 Title - enter MR, MRS, MISS, MS or other title

Mr.

Surname or family name

Singh

First or given name(s)

Upjeet

7 Last entries on P11 *Deductions Working Sheet*.
Complete only if Tax Code is cumulative. If there is an 'X' at box 6 there will be no entries here.

Week number 24   Month number ☐

Total pay to date

£ 6360.30 p

Total tax to date

£ 348.00 p

4 Leaving date *DD MM YYYY*

17 09 2014

To the new employer Complete boxes 8 to 18 and send P45 Part 3 only to your HMRC office immediately.

8 New Employer PAYE reference

Office number   *Reference number*

☐ / ☐

9 Date new employment started *DD MM YYYY*

☐ ☐ ☐

10 Works number/Payroll number and Department or branch (if any)

11 Enter 'P' here if employee will not be paid by you between the date employment began and the next 5 April.   ☐

12 Enter Tax Code in use if different to the Tax Code at box 6.

If week 1 or month 1 applies, enter 'X' in the box below.

Week 1/Month 1   ☐

13 If the tax figure you are entering on P11 *Deductions Working Sheet* differs from box 7 (see the E13 *Employer Helpbook Day-to-day payroll*) please enter the figure here.

£ ☐ p

14 New employee's job title or job description

15 Employee's private address

Postcode

16 Gender. Enter 'X' in the appropriate box

Male ☐   Female ☐

17 Date of birth *DD MM YYYY*

☐ ☐ ☐

Declaration

18 I have prepared a P11 *Deductions Working Sheet* in accordance with the details above.

Employer name and address

Postcode

Date *DD MM YYYY*

☐ ☐ ☐

P45(Online) Part 3

HMRC 10/08

Task 16

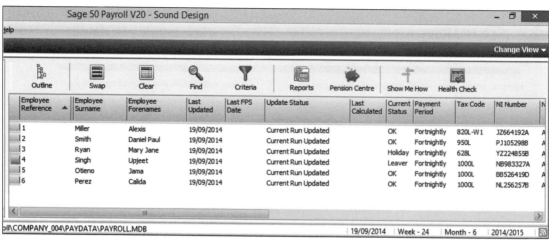

Employee Reference ▲	Employee Surname	Employee Forenames	Last Updated	Last FPS Date	Update Status	Last Calculated	Current Status	Payment Period	Tax Code	NI Number	N
1	Miller	Alexis	19/09/2014		Current Run Updated		OK	Fortnightly	820L-W1	JZ664192A	A
2	Smith	Daniel Paul	19/09/2014		Current Run Updated		OK	Fortnightly	950L	PJ1105298B	A
3	Ryan	Mary Jane	19/09/2014		Current Run Updated		Holiday	Fortnightly	628L	YZ224855B	A
4	Singh	Upjeet	19/09/2014		Current Run Updated		Leaver	Fortnightly	1000L	NB983327A	A
5	Otieno	Jama	19/09/2014		Current Run Updated		OK	Fortnightly	1000L	BB526419D	A
6	Perez	Calida	19/09/2014		Current Run Updated		OK	Fortnightly	1000L	NL256257B	A

ll\COMPANY_004\PAYDATA\PAYROLL.MDB | 19/09/2014 | Week - 24 | Month - 6 | 2014/2015

Date :

Time :

Page : 1 of 1

Sound Design
Form P32 (2014) - Employer Payment Record

Tax Month From:	6	Tax Month To:	6
Date From:	06/09/2014	Date To:	05/10/2014

1 - PAYE Income Tax:	272.00	
2 - Student Loan Deductions:	30.00	
3 - Net Income Tax:	302.00	(1 + 2)
4 - Gross National Insurance:	434.44	
5 - Employment Allowance:	0.00	
6 - Total SMP Recovered:	0.00	
7 - NIC Compensation on SMP (if due):	0.00	
8 - Total SPP Recovered:	0.00	
9 - NIC Compensation on SPP (if due):	0.00	
10 - Total ASPP Recovered:	0.00	
11 - NIC Compensation on ASPP (if due):	0.00	
12 - Total SAP Recovered:	0.00	
13 - NIC Compensation on SAP (if due):	0.00	
14 - Total NIC Deductions:	0.00	
15 - Net National Insurance:	434.44	(4 minus 5 minus 14)
16 - Employer NI to Pay:	232.36	
17 - Total Amount Due:	736.44	(3 + 15)

Note: If any values are displayed below, you must submit an Employer's Payment Summary (EPS) to HMRC.

Tax Refund Received	0.00
SSP/SMP/SPP/SAP Funding Received	0.00
Total SMP	0.00
Total SPP	0.00
Total ASPP	0.00
Total SAP	0.00
Small Employer Statutory NIC Compensation Percentage	3.00 %

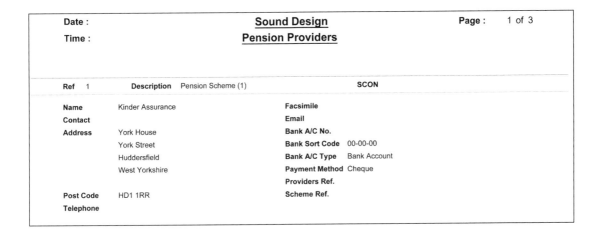

Date :	**Sound Design**	Page :	1 of 1
Time :	**Attachment History**		

	Employee Ref From :	1	Process Date From :	06/04/2014
	Employee Ref To :	9,999,999	Process Date To :	05/04/2015

EMPLOYEE :   6 - C   Perez

1 - Council Tax

Process Date	Attachable Earnings This Period	Total Value Of Attachment	Paid This Period	Paid To Date	Admin Cost This Period
19/09/2014	497.20	776.20	59.66	59.66	0.00

Date :	**Sound Design**	Page :	1 of 3
Time :	**Pension Providers**		

Ref 1	**Description** Pension Scheme (1)		**SCON**
Name	Kinder Assurance	**Facsimile**	
Contact		**Email**	
Address	York House	**Bank A/C No.**	
	York Street	**Bank Sort Code**	00-00-00
	Huddersfield	**Bank A/C Type**	Bank Account
	West Yorkshire	**Payment Method**	Cheque
		Providers Ref.	
Post Code	HD1 1RR	**Scheme Ref.**	
Telephone			

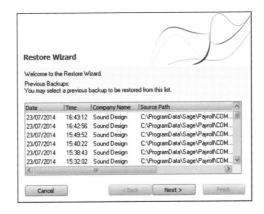

Index

for your notes

for your notes